A Scholarship Vocabulary Program

COURSE III

HAROLD LEVINE
Chairman Emeritus of English,
Benjamin Cardozo High School, New York

NORMAN LEVINE
Associate Professor of English,
City College of the City University of New York

ROBERT T. LEVINE
Professor of English,
North Carolina A & T State University

Dedicated to serving

our nation's youth

AMSCO SCHOOL PUBLICATIONS, INC.
315 Hudson Street / New York, N.Y. 10013

Vocabulary books by the authors

Vocabulary and Composition Through Pleasurable Reading,
Books I–VI
Vocabulary for Enjoyment, Books I–III
Vocabulary for the High School Student, Books A, B
Vocabulary for the High School Student
Vocabulary for the College-Bound Student
The Joy of Vocabulary
A Scholarship Vocabulary Program, Courses I–III

When ordering this book, please specify
either **R 619 S** or A SCHOLARSHIP VOCABULARY PROGRAM, COURSE III

ISBN 1-56765-022-8
NYC Item 56765-022-7

Printed in the United State of America
1 2 3 4 5 6 7 8 9 10   00 99 98 97 96 95 94

To the Student

Course III, like its predecessors in the Scholarship Vocabulary Program, teaches not only words but skills—especially the skills of close reading, critical thinking, and concise writing.

Each time you meet a lesson word in this book, you will be called upon to complete a sentence—not with the lesson word but with some other missing word. This, though you may not think so at first, requires close reading and critical thinking. Try to do what you are asked to do on page 1, and see if you don't agree. Then, for an example of a different way in which the book teaches these same skills, see page 42.

Concise writing is still another skill you will be learning in every lesson in this vocabulary book. The fastest way to learn what this skill is about is to turn now to the first concise writing exercise on page 9.

By the time you finish the book, you will have had hundreds of opportunities to perfect your reading, writing, and thinking skills—and you also will have learned many hundreds of useful words that belong in a well-educated person's vocabulary. Take a minute now to skim the Vocabulary Index, beginning with page 148.

You will find ample provision for review within each regular lesson. Note, too, that every fifth lesson is a review of the previous four lessons.

Analogy questions have been included at the end of each regular lesson, in part, because they help with the review of lesson words and their synonyms, but more importantly because they stimulate critical thinking, a principal concern of this book.

The Authors

Contents

LESSON 1

LESSON WORDS 1–10: Pronounce the word, spell it, study its meanings, and finish the sentence that follows it. See 1, below.

allegiance (*n.*) devotion to a person, group, or cause; **loyalty**; ə-ˈlē-jən(t)s **faithfulness**

1. When I rooted for the (home, visiting) __visiting__ team, some accused me of a lack of *allegiance*.

ambiguous (*adj.*) having two or more possible meanings or inter- am-ˈbig-yə-wəs pretations; hard to understand; **obscure**; **indistinct**

2. If the directions say to be sure to (stop, turn) _____ at the intersection, they are *ambiguous*.

ardent (*adj.*) characterized by warmth of feeling; **fervent**; **enthusiastic**; **devoted** ˈärd-ᵊnt

3. The candidate was noisily (cheered, booed) _____ by her *ardent* supporters.

expertise (*n.*) expert skill or knowledge; **ability**; **expertness**; ˌek-spər-ˈtēz **know-how**

4. A (coach, tyro) _____ cannot be expected to have much *expertise*.

explicit (*adj.*) fully and clearly expressed, leaving no question as ik-ˈsplis-ət to meaning or intent; **definite**; **precise**; **unambiguous**

5. It would be (hard, easy) _____ to misinterpret these instructions because they are so *explicit*.

foment (*v.*) stir up; **incite**; **instigate**; **provoke** fō-ˈment

6. There were some (cordial, malevolent) _____ individuals at the public hearing who sought to *foment* discord.

1

fortuitous (*adj.*)   occurring or produced by chance; **accidental**;
fȯr-'tü-ət-əs   **casual**

> 7. Their meeting at the library was entirely *fortuitous*; they
> (had, hadn't) _____ planned to get together.

inflammatory (*adj.*)   tending to excite anger, disorder, or tumult;
in-'flam-ə-ˌtȯr-ē   **incendiary**; **seditious**

> 8. *Inflammatory* language on both sides tended to (retard,
> accelerate) _____ the peace negotiations.

insupportable (*adj.*)   more than can be endured; **intolerable**;
ˌin-sə-'pȯrt-ə-bəl   **unbearable**

> 9. Fortunately, the pain (intensified, subsided) _____,
> or it might have become *insupportable*.

levy (*n.*)   money raised or collected by legal authority or force;
'lev-ē   **tax**; **impost**; **assessment**

> 10. The new *levy* on petroleum will probably (lower, raise)
> _____ prices at the gas pump.

SENTENCE COMPLETION 1–10: Enter the required lesson
words, as in 1, below.

---

1. The people were already so heavily taxed that a further hike

   in the sales __**levy**_____ would have been

   __**insupportable**_____ .

2. By his _____ remarks to the crowd at Caesar's

   funeral, Mark Antony _____ a revolt against

   Caesar's assassins.

3. Pat found one of my sentences _____, though

   it had seemed clear to me, and she insisted that I make it more

   _____.

4. We have been _____ fans of the Bulldogs, but

   if they continue to lose game after game some of us may transfer

   our _____ to another team.

5. The outcome of an honestly run lottery is _____;

   no _____ is needed to be a winner, just luck.

 SYNONYM ROUNDUP 1–10: Each line, when completed, should have three synonyms. Enter the missing letters, as in 1, below.

---

1. t **a** x   l **e** vy   imp **o** st

2. know-h __ w   ab __ l __ ty   experti __ __

3. ac __ idental   cas __ al   fort __ __ tous

4. f __ __ thfulness   alleg __ __ nce   l __ y __ lty

5. f __ ment   inc __ te   inst __ g __ te

6. obsc __ re   __ __ distinct   ambig __ __ us

7. __ __ support __ ble   unb __ __ rable   int __ ler __ ble

8. f __ rvent   d __ v __ ted   __ rdent

9. def __ n __ te   __ __ ambiguous   expl __ c __ t

10. infl __ mmat __ ry   s __ d __ tious   incend __ __ ry

LESSON WORDS 11–20: Pronounce the word, spell it, study its meanings, and finish the sentence that follows it.

onus (*n.*) **burden**; **obligation**; **responsibility**; disagreeable
ˈo-nəs   necessity

> 11. When charges are brought, the *onus* of proving them is
>
> on the (defendant, accuser) _____ .

pare (*v.*) cut back an outside, excess, or irregular part; **peel**;
ˈpe(ə)r   **trim**; **reduce**

> 12. The company *pared* its staff by (firing, hiring) _____
> seven workers.

pecuniary (*adj.*) pertaining to or consisting of money; **mone-**
pi-ˈkyü-nē-ˌer-ē   **tary**; **financial**

> 13. (Spendthrifts, Accountants) _____
> lack expertise in *pecuniary* matters.

petition (*n.*) formal request to a person or group in authority;
pə-ˈtish-ən   **suit**; **complaint**

> 14. My signature on the *petition* shows that I (support, op-
>
> pose) _____ it.

presentable (*adj.*) proper or suitable in attire or appearance for
pri-ˈzent-ə-bəl   being seen by others; **respectable**; **decent**

> 15. Before participating in a (telephone, face-to-face)
>
> _____ conversation with a job inter-
> viewer, make sure you look *presentable*.

proclivity (*n.*) natural or habitual inclination or tendency, espe-
prō-ˈkliv-ət-ē   cially toward something objectionable; **bent**;
    leaning; **disposition**

> 16. Fiery-tempered people have a *proclivity* for being (quick,
>
> slow) _____ to take offense.

provisional (*adj.*) serving for the time being until permanently
prə-ˈvizh-ən-ᵊl   or properly replaced; **temporary**; **makeshift**

    17. The *provisional* government will go (into, out of)

            _____ existence once the constitution is adopted
and elections are held.

redress (*v.*) set right; remove the cause of; **remedy**; **correct**
ri-ˈdres

    18. In a totalitarian state, people are (prone, loath) _____
to ask their government to *redress* their grievances.

reprehensible (*adj.*) deserving of reproof; **blameworthy**; **cen-
ˌrep-ri-ˈhen-sə-bəl   surable**

    19. It is utterly *reprehensible* to (hurt, protect) _____
the defenseless.

upbraid (*v.*) find fault with or criticize severely; **scold**; **cen-
ˌəp-ˈbrād   sure**

    20. The (lax, conscientious) _____
babysitter should not have been *upbraided*.

SENTENCE COMPLETION 11–20: Enter the required lesson words from D, above.

---

1. The bureau chiefs were _____ for overspend-

  ing, and ordered to _____ their expenditures

  in next year's budget by at least twenty percent.

2. The _____ that the colonists had sent to the

  king, asking him to _____ their grievances,

  was coldly received.

3. It is _____ for a public official nego-

tiating a contract for the government to gain any personal

_____ benefit from the transaction.

4. The individual serving as _____ com-

missioner is unlikely to get that post because of his

_____ for irritating community leaders.

5. Let us all pitch in to make this place look _____,

instead of putting the _____ solely on one

member's shoulders.

SYNONYM ROUNDUP 11–20: Each line, when completed, should have three words similar in meaning. Enter the missing letters.

---

11. c __ rrect   r __ m __ dy   __ __ dress

12. r __ duce   tr __ m   p __ re

13. cens __ re   upbr __ __ d   sc __ ld

14. b __ rden   on __ s   respons __ b __ l __ ty

15. compl __ __ nt   p __ t __ tion   s __ __ t

16. disp __ sition   procl __ v __ ty   b __ nt

17. present __ ble   d __ c __ nt   respect __ ble

18. blamew __ __ thy   censur __ ble   __ __ prehensible

19. pec __ n __ __ ry   mon __ tary   financ __ __ l

20. temp __ rary   m __ kesh __ ft   __ __ __ visional

SYNONYMS: To avoid repetition, replace the boldfaced word with a synonym from the vocabulary list below. See 1 below.

burden	**decent**
precise	**incendiary**
temporary	**peel**
impost	**ability**
enthusiastic	**blameworthy**

1. Some bystanders severely reprehended the pranksters, who at first seemed to think that what they had done was not **reprehensible**.

1. __**blameworthy**__

2. The insurance company provided funds for **provisional** living quarters for the family that had been burned out of their home.

2. _____

3. Parents want their children to look reasonably **presentable** before presenting them to visitors.

3. _____

4. The fictional Sherlock Holmes was an expert sleuth whose **expertise** was greater than that of any other crimefighter.

4. _____

5. We **pared** the potatoes with a paring knife.

5. _____**ed**

6. The opposition leader's **inflammatory** speech inflamed the passions of the audience.

6. _____

7. Everything in the instructions is explicitly explained in the most **explicit** terms.

7. _____

8. Now, the **onus** of submitting detailed monthly reports has been added to our already onerous other duties.

8. _____

9. Despite the mishap, Olga's ardor for winter sports is undi-

minished; she is as **ardent** a
skier as ever.

9. _____

10. In addition to levying a host of
nuisance taxes, the legislature is
considering a higher **levy** on
imports.

10. _____

 ANTONYMS: In the blank space in each sentence below,
enter the word most nearly the antonym of the boldfaced
word. Choose your antonyms from the following list. See 1
below.

---

unkempt	permanently
blameless	unremedied
unambiguous	cool
quell	deliberately
indefinite	disinclination

1. Some of the grievances have been **redressed**, but others re-

   main ____**unremedied**____ .

2. Those who are hired **provisionally** have much less job pro-

   tection than those who have been appointed _____ .

3. Those you say are **reprehensible** angrily protest that they are

   _____ .

4. Some who prefer not to be **explicit** when asked for their age

   give a(n) _____ answer, like "21 plus."

5. The former owner had a **proclivity** for arguing with cus-

   tomers; the new one shows a(n) _____ for
   such wrangling.

6. You were so _____ before you washed up,
   but now you look **presentable**.

7. The queen took immediate steps to _____
   the uprising that her foes had **fomented**.

8. Their intentions seem **obscure**. Why don't they state what they

   plan to do in _____ language?

9. Two of the candidate's **ardent** supporters turned _____ once they realized they had over-estimated his chances of winning.

10. The forest fire may have started **fortuitously**, perhaps from lightning, but many suspect it was set _____.

 CONCISE WRITING: Express the thought of each sentence in NO MORE THAN FOUR WORDS. See 1, below.

1. Some of the discoveries that are made are the product of chance.

   Some discoveries are fortuitous.

2. Which of the conditions that were felt to be grounds for complaint were set right?

   _____

3. The statement that you made seems to have two possible meanings.

   _____

4. The speeches that he has been delivering tend to arouse people to anger and disorder.

   _____

5. Her appointment is for the time being only, with the likelihood that she will be replaced when a permanent appointment is made to her position.

   _____

6. At all times express yourself fully and clearly, so that there will be no question in anyone's mind as to what your meaning or intention is.

   _____

ANALOGIES: Which lettered pair of words—**a, b, c, d,** or **e**—most nearly has the same relationship as the numbered pair? Enter the letter of your answer in the space provided. The first analogy question has been answered and explained as a sample.

1. FAITHLESS : ALLEGIANCE

    a. autonomous : freedom   *b.* haughty : self-importance
    c. drowsy : sleep   *d.* articulate : eloquence
    e. indignant : provocation   1. __*c*__

    Explanation: A FAITHLESS person lacks ALLEGIANCE. A **drowsy** person lacks **sleep**.

2. ARDENT : ENTHUSIASM

    a. malevolent : ill will   *b.* witless : sagacity
    c. vindictive : forgiveness   *d.* unendorsed : backing
    e. unambitious : aspiration   2. _____

    Hint: An ARDENT person is full of ENTHUSIASM.

3. UNJUST : REDRESS

    a. adequate : increase   *b.* fallacious : correct
    c. manifest : explain   *d.* crucial : ignore
    e. bleak : hope   3. _____

    Hint: Something UNJUST should be REDRESSED.

4. FISCAL : PECUNIARY

    a. inevitable : avoidable   *b.* untold : incalculable
    c. inane : significant   *d.* requisite : unnecessary
    e. drab : cheerful   4. _____

5. INSUPPORTABLE : ENDURE

    a. remediable : improve   *b.* logical : grasp
    c. warranted : excuse   *d.* reversible : change
    e. outrageous : condone   5. _____

6. PETITIONER : COMPLAIN

    a. diehard : yield   *b.* pharmacist : prescribe
    c. instigator : foment   *d.* shirker : work
    e. mutineer : comply   6. _____

7. ONUS : DUTY

    a. ordeal : experience   *b.* trifle : quantity
    c. scratch : injury   *d.* snack : meal
    e. moment : interval   7. _____

    Hint: An ONUS is a disagreeable DUTY.

8. AMBIGUITY : COMMUNICATION

    a. injury : pain   *b.* oversight : embarrassment
    c. affront : resentment   *d.* glare : visibility
    e. acquittal : rejoicing   8. _____

9. REPREHENSIBLE : UPBRAID

    a. competent : assist   *b.* humane : admire
    c. unselfish : censure   *d.* fatuous : commend
    e. gluttonous : emulate   9. _____

10. ACCIDENT : FORTUITOUS

    a. avarice : praiseworthy   *b.* indolence : exemplary
    c. mortification : painless   *d.* failure : gratifying
    e. sneezing : involuntary   10. _____

LESSON 2

LESSON WORDS 1–10: Pronounce the word, spell it, study its meanings, and finish the sentence that follows it.

---

access (*n.*)   ability, permission, or liberty to enter, approach, com-
'ak-₁ses   municate with, or use; **admittance**; **entry**

    1. (Landlocked, Island) _____ nations lack
       direct *access* to the sea.

bristle (*v.*)   become rigid with anger or irritation; **fume**; **seethe**
'bris-əl

    2. The mechanic *bristled* at the suggestion that he had done

       an (outstanding, inadequate) _____ job.

brook (*v.*)   stand for; **tolerate**; **bear**
'bru̇k

    3. They want us to be (critical, silent) _____;
       they will *brook* no interference with their plans.

capricious (*adj.*)   tending to change abruptly and without appar-
kə-'prish-əs   ent reason; **fickle**; **inconstant**; **impulsive**;
              unpredictable

    4. A *capricious* friend can (always, never) _____
       be depended on.

certitude (*n.*)   freedom from doubt; **certainty**; **conviction**;
'sərt-ə-₁tüd   **assurance**

    5. On the basis of the (pain in, X-ray of) _____
       my leg, my physician could say with *certitude* that I had
       sustained a fracture.

complicity (*n.*)   participation or involvement in a wrongful act;
kəm-'plis-ət-ē   **collusion**; **connivance**

> 6. Two were (convicted, acquitted) _____
> because of their *complicity* in the fraud.

distraught (*adj.*)   deeply agitated; **tormented**; **troubled**
dis-'tròt

> 7. If their young child had been (commended, hurt)
> _____, the parents would have been *distraught*.

impeccable (*adj.*)   free from fault or blame; **irreproachable**;
im-'pek-ə-bəl   **flawless**

> 8. Employees whose work is *impeccable* deserve no (thanks,
> rebuke) _____.

imperturbable (*adj.*)   not easily excited; **calm**; **unruffled**; **un-**
ˌim-pər-'tər-bə-bəl   **flappable**

> 9. The candidate seems *imperturbable*, but her advisers are
> (worried, confident) _____.

jubilant (*adj.*)   showing or expressing great joy; **exultant**;
'jü-bə-lənt   **triumphant**

> 10. The team that (lost, won) _____ was *jubilant*.

SENTENCE COMPLETION 1–10: Enter the required lesson
words.

---

1. We were incredulous when an official with a(n) _____

   record was accused of _____ with criminals

   to defraud the city.

2. The crew became _____ when day after day

   passed with no sight of land, but their _____

   admiral was determined to sail on.

3. The queen _____**d** when someone seemed to question her authority, and she made it perfectly clear that she would _____ no opposition.

4. The refugees were _____ when they learned that their _____ to asylum would not be blocked.

5. There is no _____ that those who promised to vote for Diana will do so; many people are _____ .

 SYNONYM ROUNDUP 1–10: Each line, when completed, should have three synonyms. Enter the missing letters.

---

1. t __ rmented   tr __ __ bled   distr __ __ ght

2. admitt __ nce   entr __   ac __ __ ss

3. t __ l __ rate   br __ __ k   b __ __ r

4. fl __ wless   irrepr __ __ chable   __ __ peccable

5. tri __ mphant   jub __ lant   ex __ ltant

6. br __ stle   f __ me   s __ __ the

7. capric __ __ us   fic __ le   unpredict __ ble

8. ass __ rance   cert __ t __ de   conv __ ction

9. coll __ sion   conn __ vance   compl __ c __ ty

10. c __ lm   impert __ rbable   unfl __ pp __ ble

	LESSON WORDS 11–20: Pronounce the word, spell it, study its meanings, and finish the sentence that follows it.
D	

---

mollify (*v.*) soothe in temper or disposition; **pacify**; **placate**;
'mäl-ə-ˌfī   **appease**

   11. The manager tried to *mollify* the (contented, irate) _____ customer.

nadir (*n.*) lowest point; **bottom**; **low**
'nā-ˌdi(ə)r

   12. The Wildcats' luck was at its *nadir* when they found themselves in sole possession of (last, first) _____ place.

nettle (*v.*) arouse to sharp but brief annoyance or anger; **irri-**
'net-ᵊl   **tate**; **provoke**; **exasperate**

   13. A hot-headed person is (rarely, easily) _____ *nettled*.

pinnacle (*n.*) highest point of achievement or development;
'pin-i-kəl   **summit**; **zenith**; **apex**

   14. Bad weather impeded the climbers in their (ascent, descent) _____ to the *pinnacle*.

rash (*n.*) large number of instances in a small period; **epidemic**;
'rash   **outbreak**; **plague**

   15. It is prudent to (take, avoid) _____ a route noted for a *rash* of recent accidents.

staunch (*adj.*) steadfast in loyalty or principle; **faithful**; **con-**
'stónch   **stant**

   16. Our *staunch* ally gave us (lukewarm, wholehearted) _____ support.

superlative (*adj.*) of the highest kind or order; **superb**; **out-**
sủ-'pər-lət-iv   **standing**

17. Everyone on the staff was highly (proficient, incompetent)

_____; the service was *superlative*.

tortuous (*adj.*)   full of twists, turns, or bends; **winding**; **serpen-**
ˈtórch-ə-wəs   **tine**

18. A driver on that *tortuous* road (constantly, rarely)

_____ has to turn the steering wheel.

universal (*adj.*)   existing or prevailing everywhere; **worldwide**;
ˌyü-nə-ˈvər-səl   **global**

19. The gymnast is (hardly, well) _____ known outside her own country; her fame is *universal*.

virulent (*adj.*)   extremely poisonous or venomous; **noxious**;
ˈvir-yə-lənt   **toxic**

20. To most people, the sting of a (rattlesnake, rebuke)

_____ may be painful but not partic-
ularly *virulent*.

  SENTENCE COMPLETION 11–20: Enter the required lesson words from D, above.

---

1. My sister was so _____**d** by my criticism of her Hal-

loween costume that I could do nothing to _____ her.

2. When the ousted executive was at the _____ of his for-

tunes, he was abandoned by all but a few _____

friends.

3. There has been a _____ of collisions on a _____

stretch of the highway where many drivers disregard the posted

speed limits.

4. For her _____ record at the 1976 Olym-

   pics, when she was only fourteen, the Romanian gymnast Nadia

   Comaneci won _____ acclaim.

5. Alexander the Great was only 33 when he died of a _____

   fever at the _____ of his career.

SYNONYM ROUNDUP 11–20: Each line, when completed, should have three synonyms. Enter the missing letters.

---

11. s __ mmit   ap __ x   p __ nn __ cle

12. st __ __ nch   f __ __ thful   const __ nt

13. bott __ m   l __ w   nad __ r

14. worldw __ de   un __ versal   gl __ b __ l

15. irr __ t __ te   ex __ sperate   n __ ttle

16. r __ sh   outbr __ __ k   ep __ d __ mic

17. nox __ __ us   t __ xic   v __ r __ lent

18. sup __ rb   s __ perl __ tive   __ __ __ standing

19. pl __ cate   moll __ fy   app __ __ se

20. w __ nding   s __ rp __ ntine   tort __ ous

SYNONYMS: To avoid repetition, replace the boldfaced word with a synonym from the vocabulary list below.

**irritate   nadir   unruffled   pacify   superb
certainty   serpentine   global   distraught   entry**

1. One company stands head and shoulders above its competitors; its products are **outstanding**.

2. If the building is inaccessible from the main entrance because of repairs, you can gain **access** from the delivery entrance.

3. The problem is nettlesome, but it eventually will be solved; in the meantime, don't let it **nettle** you.

4. There is a **worldwide** demand for American products; they are used all over the world.

5. Experts believed that the recession was bottoming out and that we were already at or near its **bottom**.

6. Some will not leave their homes because they are sure they can ride out the storm, but there is no **assurance** they will be able to do so.

7. He seemed **troubled**, but we couldn't tell what was troubling him.

8. The parents tried to **mollify** the crying infant with a toy, but he refused to be mollified.

9. We were on a **winding** road that kept winding into and out of the sunlight, but fortunately we had our sunglasses.

10. If our guide was perturbed by the change in the weather, she didn't show it; she seemed **imperturbable**.

1. _____

2. _____

3. _____

4. _____

5. _____

6. _____

7. _____

8. _____

9. _____

10. _____

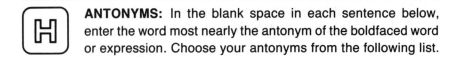

ANTONYMS: In the blank space in each sentence below, enter the word most nearly the antonym of the boldfaced word or expression. Choose your antonyms from the following list.

exasperate	constant
touchy	straight
zenith	conviction
nonpoisonous	miserable
defective	bristled

1. Though most protesters **did not get angry** when asked to move on, a few of them _____.

2. We were _____ when our candidates were defeated, but those who had opposed them were **jubilant**.

3. The manager's attempt to **placate** the customers served only to _____ them.

4. It is hard to believe that a **virulent** substance like asbestos was for many years treated as _____.

5. The day he was swept into office by a landslide was the _____ of the legislator's career, and the day he was forced to resign was its **nadir**.

6. Though we tried our best, we have no _____ that what we did was right, and we face the future with **uncertainty**.

7. One would expect a brand new lamp to be in **impeccable** condition, yet the one I just bought had a(n) _____ switch.

8. The chief is **unflappable**, but his deputies are _____; they take offense at the slightest provocation.

9. We have members who are so **capricious** that one cannot tell where they stand at a given moment; they are not _____ in their views.

10. There are two routes; one is **tortuous** but very scenic; the other is _____ and will get you to your destination faster.

CONCISE WRITING: Express the thought of each sentence in NO MORE THAN FOUR WORDS.

1. Pollution can be found in every part of the world.

_____

2. The planning that they did was of the highest order.

_____

3. He had the appearance of someone who was deeply agitated.

_____

4. No one could possibly have found any fault at all with the performance that she gave.

_____

5. Participation or involvement in the commission of a wrongful act is something that we cannot treat as trivial, harmless, or unimportant.

_____

ANALOGIES: Which lettered pair of words—**a, b, c, d,** or **e**—most nearly has the same relationship as the numbered pair? Enter the letter of your answer in the space provided.

1. ROAD : ACCESS

   a. bridge : maintenance   *b.* furnace : basement
   c. plane : hangar   *d.* dwelling : shelter
   e. refrigerator : spoilage   1. _____

2. IMPERTURBABLE : BRISTLE

   a. indulgent : forgive   *b.* adamant : resist
   c. unwavering : hesitate   *d.* tractable : comply
   e. loquacious : talk   2. _____

3. SUPERLATIVE : ADMIRATION

    a. reprehensible : commendation   *b.* trivial : consideration
    c. mediocre : emulation   *d.* perfect : repair
    e. outrageous : denunciation   3. _____

4. BROOK : TOLERATE

    a. redress : correct   *b.* ban : permit
    c. despise : revere   *d.* disparage : laud
    e. fill : deplete   4. _____

5. VIRULENT : POISONOUS

    a. semiprecious : valuable   *b.* economical : costly
    c. lukewarm : hot   *d.* crucial : important
    e. inferior : praiseworthy   5. _____

6. STAUNCH : ALLEGIANCE

    a. gluttonous : self-control   *b.* unrepentant : remorse
    c. aimless : direction   *d.* malicious : goodwill
    e. persistent : goal   6. _____

7. PEACEMAKER : MOLLIFY

    a. scoffer : approve   *b.* consultant : advise
    c. customer : serve   *d.* skinflint : share
    e. expediter : obstruct   7. _____

8. VICTORY : EXULTANT

    a. failure : jubilant   *b.* illness : robust
    c. foreboding : uneasy   *d.* exercise : affluent
    e. blunder : proud   8. _____

9. CERTITUDE : DOUBT

    a. indolence : sloth   *b.* impost : levy
    c. independence : autonomy   *d.* candor : evasiveness
    e. complicity : connivance   9. _____

10. ACCESSIBLE : REACH

    a. inevitable : avoid   *b.* peerless : match
    c. unwarranted : justify   *d.* mortifying : endure
    e. unambiguous : understand   10. _____

LESSON 3

LESSON WORDS 1–10: Pronounce the word, spell it, study its meanings, and finish the sentence that follows it.

---

abrogate (*v.*)   abolish by formal action; **annul**; **nullify**; **invali-**
'ab-rə-'gāt   **date**

    1. Public reaction to the new law was so (favorable, critical)

    _____ that the legislature voted to *ab-rogate* it.

allay (*v.*)   put to rest; **calm**; **quiet**
ə-'lā

    2. To *allay* the (support, suspicion) _____
    of the company's president, the treasurer offered to take
    a lie-detector test.

bizarre (*adj.*)   strikingly out of the ordinary; **odd**; **strange**
bə-'zär

    3. A magazine specializing in coverage of *bizarre* events sent
    a reporter to investigate the rumored (trout, monster)

    _____ in the lake.

brash (*adj.*)   heedless of the consequences; **audacious**; **reck-**
'brash   **less**; **foolhardy**

    4. The *brash* new supervisor (fired, praised) _____
    three assistants the very first day.

confront (*v.*)   stand or come in front of; **meet**; **face**
kən-'frənt

    5. It is better for us to *confront* our problems rather than to

    try to (ignore, resolve) _____ them.

diminutive (*adj.*)   of relatively small size; **small**; **little**; **tiny**
də-'min-yət-iv

6. The *diminutive* batter astonished the crowd by hitting the ball over the head of the (center fielder, pitcher) _____ .

dismantle (*v.*) take apart; **destroy**; **demolish**
dis-'mant-ºl

7. The news that the luxury hotel built (two, sixty) _____ years ago is soon to be *dismantled* seems utterly bizarre.

havoc (*n.*) wide and general destruction; **devastation**; **ruin**
'hav-ik

8. A(n) (artificial, real) _____ bull would create *havoc* in the glassware department.

horrify (*v.*) cause to feel horror; **dismay**; **appall**
'hór-ə-ˌfī
  or 'här-ə-ˌfī

9. Millions were *horrified* by the (lives, property) _____ lost when the Titanic, with 2200 aboard, hit an iceberg and sank in 1912.

inordinate (*adj.*) not within proper limits; **immoderate**; **ex-**
in-'órd-ºn-ət   **cessive**

10. Customers were (pleased, exasperated) _____ by the *inordinate* increase in prices.

SENTENCE COMPLETION 1–10: Enter the required lesson words.

1. Gulliver found himself in the _____ situation

of being tied down to the ground with scores of _____ warriors clambering over his body.

2. After _____ing the Russians' suspicions by signing

a nonaggression pact with them, Hitler proceeded to _____ that treaty by invading Russia.

3. The amazed spectators must have thought it was _____

of David, a mere boy, to _____ the giant Goliath.

4. Authorities subjected motorists to _____ delays

by closing the parkway so that workers could _____

and remove a wrecked trailer.

5. In 1976, the world was _____**ed** to learn of the

_____ and monumental loss of life caused by an

earthquake in Northeastern China.

SYNONYM ROUNDUP 1–10: Each line, when completed, should have three synonyms. Enter the missing letters.

---

1. f __ ce	m __ __ t	confr __ nt
2. hav __ c	ru __ n	dev __ station
3. b __ z __ rre	__ dd	str __ nge
4. d __ stroy	d __ m __ lish	__ __ __ mantle
5. qu __ et	__ __ lay	__ alm
6. exc __ ssive	__ __ moderate	__ __ ordinate
7. __ rash	r __ ckless	__ __ dacious
8. dism __ y	h __ rr __ fy	app __ ll
9. sm __ ll	d __ min __ tive	litt __ __
10. n __ llify	abr __ gate	ann __ l

LESSON WORDS 11–20: Pronounce the word, spell it, study its meanings, and finish the sentence that follows it.

---

insatiable (*adj.*)   incapable of being satisfied; **quenchless**; **un-**
in-'sā-shə-bəl   **appeasable**

11. "(Enough, More) _____ food!" cried the *insatiable* eater.

irrepressible (*adj.*)   incapable of being restrained; **uncontrol-**
ir-i-'pres-ə-bəl   **lable**; **insuppressible**

12. There was (prolonged, scant) _____ applause from the *irrepressible* audience.

irrevocable (*adj.*)   incapable of being recalled or revoked; **unal-**
ir-'rev-ə-kə-bəl   **terable**; **irreversible**

13. It is (prudent, discourteous) _____ to pause for reflection before making an *irrevocable* commitment.

mentor (*n.*)   wise and trusted counselor; **guide**; **adviser**
'men-ˌtȯr

14. For guidance in matters beyond our experience, we have (little, great) _____ need of a *mentor*.

myriad (*adj.*)   of an indefinitely large number; **innumerable**;
'mir-ē-əd   **countless**

15. (With, Without) _____ a good education, one's opportunities for advancement are *myriad*.

pandemonium (*n.*)   wild uproar; **tumult**; **hullabaloo**
ˌpan-də-'mō-nē-əm

16. The noise swiftly (grew, subsided) _____ into a *pandemonium*.

prerogative (*n.*)   special right possessed by an individual or
pri-'räg-ət-iv   group; **privilege**; **advantage**

17. Freedom of speech is a *prerogative* (denied to, enjoyed by) _____ autonomous citizens.

quip (*n.*)   witty or funny observation or response usually made on
'kwip   the spur of the moment; **joke**; **witticism**

18. *Quips* are the stock in trade of (plumbers, comedians)

_____ .

raucous (*adj.*)   disagreeably harsh in sound; **strident**; **hoarse**
ˈró-kəs

19. The music lovers in the audience were (delighted, shocked)

_____ by some of the *raucous* voices in

the chorus.

sanguine (*adj.*)   cheerful, hopeful, or confident; **optimistic**; **as-**
ˈsaŋ-gwən   **sured**

20. With our (insurmountable, thin) _____

lead, we could not feel *sanguine* about the outcome.

SENTENCE COMPLETION 11–20: Enter the required lesson words from D, above.

---

1. Dorene is grateful to her music _____**s** for having

inspired her with a(n) _____ love for the

guitar.

2. Despite the _____ problems that confront our nation,

most of us are _____ that it will survive.

3. You know, of course, that your decision to join the club is not

_____ ; you have the _____

to resign at any time.

4. Yorick's _____**s** and pranks used to make the table roar

with _____ laughter.

5. Gulls competing for scraps of food on the beach, filled the air

with their _____ cries, and the

_____ awoke us.

SYNONYM ROUNDUP 11–20: Enter the missing letters.

---

11. adv __ ser	ment __ r	g __ __ de
12. inn __ merable	c __ __ ntless	myr __ __ d
13. adv __ ntage	pr __ v __ lege	prer __ g __ tive
14. irr __ press __ ble	insuppress __ ble	uncontrol __ __ ble
15. j __ ke	q __ __ p	witt __ cism
16. qu __ nchless	unapp __ __ sable	insat __ __ ble
17. ass __ red	opt __ m __ stic	sang __ __ ne
18. t __ m __ lt	hull __ b __ loo	pand __ m __ nium
19. unalter __ ble	irr __ voc __ ble	irrevers __ ble
20. h __ __ rse	r __ __ cous	str __ dent

SYNONYMS: To avoid repetition, replace the boldfaced word
with a synonym from the vocabulary list below.

---

sanguine
small
annul
unappeasable
prerogative

face
irreversible
excessive
reckless
insuppressible

1. Lenny's **diminutive** stature in no way diminishes the team's chances for winning; in fact, he is usually the star of the game.

1. _____

2. Let us not be afraid to **confront** the truth; many of us would welcome that confrontation.

2. _____

3. Try as I might, I could not repress my yawning; it was **irrepressible**.

3. _____

4. After two helpings at the "all-you-can-eat" fish fry, I was satiated, but others with **insatiable** appetites kept eating and eating.

4. _____

5. The granting of a driver's license is not **irrevocable**; the state may at any time revoke the license for just cause.

5. _____

6. The privileged classes enjoyed **privileges** that were denied to the rest of society.

6. _____**s**

7. My mentor was sure I would do very well, though I myself felt much less **assured**.

7. _____

8. We were advised not to **abrogate** the agreement because abrogation would not have been to our advantage.

8. _____

9. Your cousins must be inordinately fond of TV because they devote an **inordinate** amount of their time to it.

9. _____

10. It is **brash** to ride a motor-
cycle without wearing the
required safety gear; such
brashness is likely to lead to
a serious accident.   10. _____

H	**ANTONYMS:** In the blank space in each sentence below, enter the word most nearly the antonym of the boldfaced word or expression. Choose your antonyms from the following list.

---

melodious ordinary quenchless quiet   repressible
intensify   avoid   alterable   reassemble reasonable

1. The onset of tears in infants is **uncontrollable,** but in adults
   it is usually _____.

2. So many of the guests at the Halloween party arrived in **bizarre** costumes that the few who had come in _____
   attire felt out of place.

3. We waited until the **pandemonium** had subsided and
   _____ was restored.

4. The assurances we were given are so ambiguous that they will
   _____ our fears—not **allay** them.

5. Hunger in the average individual is **not insatiable,** but in a
   glutton it seems _____.

6. Before signing an **irrevocable** agreement, remember that you
   will have to observe all its provisions; none of them are

   _____.

7. A severe cold can make a person with the most _____
   voice sound **raucous** on the telephone.

8. The temporary stands erected before the ceremony have been

   dismantled, but they can easily be _____**d**
   if required for a future occasion.

9. We would be willing to meet any _____ re-
   quests, but your demands are **inordinate**.

10. After my friend and I disagreed, I wanted to **confront** him to resolve our differences, but he took pains to _____ me.

CONCISE WRITING: Express the thought of each sentence in NO MORE THAN FOUR WORDS.

---

1. The dangerous situation that they were in filled us with horror.

   _____

2. Were the suspicions that you have had put to rest?

   _____

3. The witty observations and responses that she kept making on the spur of the moment were delightful.

   _____

4. Behavior that is strikingly out of the ordinary attracts attention.

   _____

5. The wise and trusted counselor who has been advising you is not one to get easily excited.

   _____

ANALOGIES: Which lettered pair of words—**a, b, c, d,** or **e**—most nearly has the same relationship as the numbered pair? Enter the letter of your answer in the space provided.

---

1. DAREDEVIL : BRASHNESS
   - *a.* drifter : ambition
   - *b.* dolt : sagacity
   - *c.* fence-sitter : indecision
   - *d.* bungler : know-how
   - *e.* sloven : neatness

   1. _____

2. ALLAY : EXCITE
   - *a.* appall : horrify
   - *b.* deride : ridicule
   - *c.* countenance : abet
   - *d.* exculpate : absolve
   - *e.* upbraid : commend

   2. _____

3. WITTICISM : AMUSE

    a. tirade : denounce   *b.* ruse : inform
    c. disparagement : laud   *d.* endorsement : harass
    e. irritation : soothe   3. _____

4. BIZARRE : NOTICE

    a. inimitable : duplicate   *b.* explicit : understand
    c. fortuitous : avoid   *d.* unfeasible : do
    e. inaccessible : approach   4. _____

5. FREEDOM OF SPEECH : PREROGATIVE

    a. publication : magazine   *b.* coin : nickel
    c. fiber : silk   *d.* injury : inflammation
    e. pine : tree   5. _____

6. INSATIABLE : SATISFY

    a. timid : coerce   *b.* opinionated : sway
    c. forgetful : remember   *d.* illiterate : write
    e. tractable : manage   6. _____

7. ABROGATE : INVALID

    a. exaggerate : truthful   *b.* facilitate : difficult
    c. elucidate : unambiguous   *d.* obstruct : accessible
    e. overlook : careless   7. _____

8. WRECKER : DISMANTLE

    a. ne'er-do-well : excel   *b.* prober : fathom
    c. defendant : accuse   *d.* narrator : listen
    e. dawdler : prosper   8. _____

9. SANGUINE : CONFIDENCE

    a. distraught : hope   *b.* proficient : expertise
    c. insolent : respect   *d.* willing : reluctance
    e. inimical : friendliness   9. _____

10. STRIDENT : EAR

    a. fragrant : nostrils   *b.* complimentary : self-image
    c. glaring : eye   *d.* delectable : tongue
    e. soothing : nerves   10. _____

LESSON 4

 LESSON WORDS 1–10: Pronounce the word, spell it, study its meanings, and finish the sentence that follows it.

alienate (*v.*)   make unfriendly, hostile, or indifferent; **estrange**;
'āl-ē-ə-ˌnāt   **disaffect**

1. A (considerate, rude) _____ person tends to *alienate* others.

captivate (*v.*)   attract and hold the attention and interest of; **fas-**
'kap-tə-ˌvāt   **cinate**; **charm**

2. (Mediocre, Inspired) _____ performances do not *captivate* audiences.

current (*adj.*)   now going on or existing; generally accepted or
'kər-ənt   prevailing at the moment; **present**; **contempo-**
rary

3. A (history textbook, daily newspaper) _____ is a good source of information about *current* events.

discretion (*n.*)   quality of being *discreet* (judicious in one's con-
dis-'kresh-ən   duct or speech, especially with regard to maintaining silence about something of a delicate nature); **prudence**; **circumspection**

4. One should never discuss (important, confidential) _____ matters with a person who lacks *discretion*.

drastic (*adj.*)   having a strong or vehement effect; **extreme**; **se-**
'dras-tik   **vere**; **harsh**

5. A (slight, huge) _____ drop in a company's an-
nual sales may require a *drastic* reduction in its work force.

duplicate (*v.*)   make an exact copy of; **imitate**; **reproduce**
'dü-pli-ˌkāt

6. Some forgers are so (adept, inept) _____ that they can almost *duplicate* a painting by Rembrandt.

evacuate (*v.*) withdraw from; **vacate**; **leave**
i-ˈvak-yə-ˌwāt

7. The heavy (fog, smoke) _____ compelled tenants to *evacuate* the building.

forbearance (*n.*) quality of being patient or self-controlled when
fȯr-ˈbe(ə)r-əns   provoked; **patience**; **leniency**

8. You don't have to ask the lender for *forbearance* if you return what you have borrowed (at, after) _____ the promised time.

futile (*adj.*) serving no useful purpose; completely ineffective;
ˈfyüt-ᵊl   **fruitless**; **vain**

9. It is *futile* to leave for a parade that will (begin, end) _____ by the time you get there.

germane (*adj.*) closely or significantly related; **relevant**; **perti-**
jər-ˈmān   **nent**

10. Since our topic is music, your remarks about your favorite (composer, dessert) _____ are not *germane*.

SENTENCE COMPLETION 1–10: Enter the required lesson words.

---

1. Our new neighbors plan to move in the day after the _____ tenants _____ the apartment.

2. It was a(n) _____ meeting; members kept bringing up matters that were not _____ , and we never got to the business we were supposed to discuss.

3. Don't _____ people who disagree with you by

immediately condemning them. Try to see things from their per-

spective. Show some _____.

4. It is a lack of _____ to take the _____

step of accusing someone of dishonesty when you have no solid

evidence—only suspicion

5. A card trick that a friend showed me _____**d**

me so much that I couldn't rest till I had learned how to

_____ it.

SYNONYM ROUNDUP 1–10: Each line, when completed, should have three synonyms. Enter the missing letters.

---

1. sev __ re   extr __ me   dr __ stic

2. ch __ rm   c __ ptivate   fas __ inate

3. pr __ s __ nt   c __ rrent   c __ __ temporary

4. im __ tate   d __ plicate   repr __ d __ ce

5. pat __ __ nce   f __ __ bearance   len __ __ ncy

6. l __ __ ve   v __ c __ te   evac __ __ te

7. germ __ ne   pert __ nent   rel __ v __ nt

8. estr __ nge   dis __ ffect   al __ __ nate

9. fru __ tless   v __ __ n   f __ t __ le

10. discr __ tion   pr __ dence   c __ rc __ mspection

LESSON WORDS 11–20: Pronounce the word, spell it, study its meanings, and finish the sentence that follows it.

mendacious (*adj.*)   given to or marked by deception, falsehood,
men-'dā-shəs   or divergence from the truth; **dishonest**;
untruthful

     11. *Mendacious* testimony can (cause, prevent) _____ a miscarriage of justice.

pique (*v.*)   arouse anger or resentment in; wound the pride of;
'pēk   **nettle**; **peeve**; **irritate**

     12. What is it that *piques* you? You seem (fatigued, annoyed)

_____ .

ponder (*v.*)   weigh carefully in the mind; **appraise**; **consider**
'pän-dər

     13. A brash person acts (after, before) _____ *pondering* the consequences.

privation (*n.*)   state of being deprived of the usual necessities of
prī-'vā-shən   life; **want**; **need**; **deprivation**

     14. There are (seldom, often) _____ occasions for rejoicing in a life of *privation*.

quagmire (*n.*)   soft, swampy ground that yields under the foot;
'kwag-ˌmī(ə)r   entrapping situation; **morass**; **predicament**

     15. A deluge turned the (paved, dirt) _____ road into a *quagmire*.

shred (*n.*)   very small piece or amount; **fragment**; **particle**;
'shred   **scrap**

     16. The probe was thorough; every *shred* of evidence was (pursued, noted) _____ .

solemn (*adj.*)   made or done seriously or thoughtfully; **serious**;
'säl-əm   **earnest**

     17. Law-enforcement officials have a *solemn* obligation to (ignore, report) _____ the offer of a bribe.

spontaneous (*adj.*)   resulting from a natural impulse or ten-
spän-'tā-nē-əs.   dency, without effort or premeditation; **un-
                       premeditated**; **instinctive**

    18. The ruthless dictator's (birthday, downfall) _____
        sparked *spontaneous* celebrations throughout the land.

status (*n.*)   position of an individual in relation to others; **rank**;
'stat-əs   **standing**

    19. A (demotion, promotion) _____ does not
        enhance one's *status.*

wrest (*v.*)   take by force or violent effort; **extort**; **wring**
'rest

    20. The front-runner's gradually (faltering, accelerating)
        _____ pace made it difficult to
        wrest the lead from her.

SENTENCE COMPLETION 11–20: Enter the required lesson words from D, above.

---

1. Rumors were circulating that the commander had been reduced

   in _____ , but there was not one _____ of

   truth in them.

2. It _____**d** me when the person who had given

   _____ assurances that she would return my notes

   the very next day failed to do so.

3. In 1789, after centuries of injustice and _____ ,

   the French people _____**ed** control of the govern-

   ment from their oppressors.

4. The investors, misled by the _____ claims

   of the swindler they had trusted, are in a _____

   from which they cannot extricate themselves.

5. When the explosion occurred, our _____

reaction was to go to the aid of the victims; there was no time to

_____ the danger to ourselves.

| F | **SYNONYM ROUNDUP 11–20:** Enter the missing letters. |

---

11. w __ nt   n __ __ d   pr __ vation

12. st __ t __ s   st __ nding   r __ nk

13. part __ cle   scr __ p   __ __ red

14. s __ rious   __ __ rnest   s __ le __ n

15. irr __ tate   p __ que   n __ ttle

16. pred __ c __ ment   __ __ agmire   m __ r __ ss

17. cons __ der   p __ nder   appr __ __ se

18. ext __ rt   wr __ st   wr __ ng

19. d __ shonest   __ __ truthful   mend __ c __ __ us

20. inst __ nctive   __ __ premeditated spontan __ __ us

| G | **SYNONYMS:** To avoid repetition, replace the boldfaced word with a synonym from the vocabulary list below. |

| serious | vain | reproduce | severe | vacate |
| morass | prudence | patience | need | scrap |

1. Despite the evacuation order, some occupants have not **evacuated** the premises.

1. _____ d

2. There is not a **shred** of truth in the rumor that the records sought by the investigators have been shredded; nothing is missing from the files.

2. _____

3. We had a hard time trying to get out of that **quagmire**; our boots and dungarees are still covered with mire.

3. _____

4. A man engaged in a **futile** attempt to catch up with the horizon was told of the futility of what he was doing, but he refused to listen.

4. _____

5. When the witness who had solemnly sworn to tell the truth became balky, the prosecutor reminded her of her **solemn** pledge.

5. _____

6. People who have never in their lives been deprived are unlikely to know what **privation** really is.

6. _____

7. Please bear with us because there is not much longer to wait; we ask for your **forbearance**.

7. _____

8. When one shop drastically lowers prices, its competitors may respond with even more **drastic** cuts.

8. _____

9. The simplest way to **duplicate** a letter is to use a duplicating machine.

9. _____

10. A discreet person like you knows when to speak and when to be silent, but unfortunately not everyone has your **discretion**.

10. _____

H

ANTONYMS: In the blank space in each sentence below, enter the word most nearly the antonym of the boldfaced word. Choose your antonyms from the following list.

abundance	premeditated
indiscretion	moderate
reconcile	repel
inflexibility	truthful
obsolete	trivial

1. The jury has to decide whether the defendant's wounding of the intruder was a(n) _____ assault or a **spontaneous** act of self-defense.

2. Long years of drought have brought **privation** to the country that once was a land of _____.

3. **Prudence** requires us to save some money for a rainy day. If we squander it, we may soon regret our _____.

4. Violence in films and TV **captivates** some people but _____s millions of others.

5. An oath is a **solemn** pledge; it must not be regarded as _____.

6. Since we did not know we were dealing with a **mendacious** person, we had no reason to believe that he was anything but _____.

7. Considering that the intractable child is so young, we believe the parent should have shown some **forbearance**, rather than _____.

8. Pam has long been **alienated** from her sister, but it seems she may soon become _____d with her.

9. Advances in medical knowledge are occurring rapidly; we should not be surprised if the **current** treatment for a disease soon becomes _____.

10. Most consider the $200 fine for overtime parking too **drastic** and think it should be replaced by a more _____ penalty.

I **CONCISE WRITING:** Express the thought of each sentence in NO MORE THAN FOUR WORDS.

1. The person who was telling stories attracted and held our attention and interest.

    _____

2. Ray likes the styles that are generally accepted at this moment in time.

    _____

3. The lack of tact that you display has the effect of making people unfriendly, hostile, or indifferent.

    _____

4. This is a situation from which it will be difficult for us to extract ourselves.

    _____

5. The officials who umpired the game demonstrated that they could be patient and maintain their self-control when provoked.

    _____
    _____

 ANALOGIES: Which lettered pair of words—**a, b, c, d,** or **e**—most nearly has the same relationship as the numbered pair? Enter the letter of your answer in the space provided.

1. FASCINATING : CAPTIVATE

    a. melancholy : gladden   *b.* trifling : deter
    c. uninteresting : bore   *d.* ordinary : inspire
    e. obnoxious : please   1. _____

2. MENDACIOUS : CANDOR

    a. sanguine : confidence   *b.* intransigent : stubbornness
    c. insatiable : appetite   *d.* inarticulate : eloquence
    e. magnanimous : generosity   2. _____

3. MORASS : ENTRAP

    a. grievance : redress   *b.* blind alley : frustrate
    c. shortcut : delay   *d.* blunder : correct
    e. chore : do   3. _____

4. GERMANE : IRRELEVANT

    a. flimsy : inadequate   *b.* tepid : unenthusiastic
    c. defunct : extinct   *d.* pardonable : condonable
    e. explicit : ambiguous   4. _____

5. NEOPHYTE : STATUS

    a. liar : credibility   *b.* graduate : diploma
    c. candidate : platform   *d.* mentor : guidance
    e. delegate : representation   5. _____

6. PREMEDITATED : SPONTANEITY

    a. chaotic : confusion   *b.* trite : originality
    c. perilous : risk   *d.* assorted : variety
    e. doubtful : uncertainty   6. _____

7. INDULGENT : FORBEARANCE

    a. restive : patience   *b.* vindictive : forgiveness
    c. penitent : remorse   *d.* composure : misgiving
    e. unqualified : competence   7. _____

8. ALIENATE : UNFRIENDLY

    a. thwart : successful   *b.* exculpate : guilty
    c. subjugate : independent   *d.* placate : angry
    e. disparage : indignant   8. _____

9. PONDER : CONSIDERATION

    a. neglect : attention   *b.* buy : ownership
    c. emulate : admiration   *d.* borrow : debt
    e. guess : evidence   9. _____

10. PIQUE : PRIDE

    a. promote : status   *b.* malign : reputation
    c. mollify : resentment   *d.* chide : disapproval
    e. spurn : ill will   10. _____

LESSON 5: REVIEW AND ENRICHMENT

CLOSE READING: Read the following statements. Then answer questions 1–10.

STATEMENTS

Falstaff, Shakespeare's most famous comic character, was known for his wit, his fondness for food and drink, and his proclivity for boasting and lying.

In the code of law drawn up by Draco in ancient Athens, almost every crime—regardless of its seriousness—was punishable by death.

When we asked Dorene whether she would be coming to our picnic, she said, "I might be there."

The company employee who had informed the suspects about the contents of the safe was not present at the time of the burglary.

Mike had changed his mind so many times for no apparent reason that those who knew him were no longer surprised by that behavior.

The director found fault with the star of the show for always being late to rehearsals.

By the time the water began to boil, the cook had finished peeling the potatoes.

After the parade, the maintenance crew took apart the reviewing stand and hauled it away to storage.

Victor Hugo's *Les Miserables* is a novel about poverty and slum life in late 18th and early 19th century France.

The first performance was sensational but, though the players subsequently tried their best, they could not repeat that opening-night triumph.

QUESTIONS

1. Who was ambiguous? _____

2. Who failed to duplicate something? _____

3. Who seemed capricious? _____

4. Who was upbraided? _____

5. Who focused attention on privation? _____

6. Who was in complicity with others? _____

7. Who pared something? _____

8. Who dismantled something? _____

9. Who prescribed a drastic remedy? _____

10. Who was mendacious? _____

CONCISE WRITING: Make the following passages more concise, using no more than the number of words suggested.

---

1. Thank you for advising me to express myself fully and clearly, so that there will be no question as to my meaning. I hope that in the directions I am enclosing, I have said nothing that can have two or more possible meanings or interpretations.   (*Cut to about 15–18 words.*)

MODEL

Thank you for advising me to be explicit. I hope nothing in the enclosed directions is ambiguous.

2. The prices that customers are being charged at this particular moment of time do not seem unreasonable.   (*Cut to 4 words.*)

_____

3. In every country in the world, even in the ones that are most prosperous, there are deprived people who are suffering from a lack of the basic necessities of life.   (*Cut to 3 words.*)

_____

4. Children who are young are not judicious enough to know when to keep silent, especially about something of a delicate or confidential nature.   (*Cut to 4 words.*)

_____

5. A circus attracts and holds the attention and interest of everyone, rich or poor, young or old.   (*Cut to 4 words.*)

_____

_____

 CLOSE READING: Read the following statements. Then answer questions 11–20.

_____

STATEMENTS

Alicia was able to persuade the personnel director to accept her application a day after the deadline.

After the disaster, the Smiths lived in a nearby motel until their apartment was ready for reoccupancy.

When the *USS Monitor*, an ironclad warship designed and built by John Ericcson, went into action, it looked to some observers like a "cheesebox on a raft."

On her birthday, Sarah had the privilege of sitting in the seat of honor, but she preferred to remain in her usual chair at the table.

The car thief zigzagged in and out of traffic lanes at high speeds in an attempt to evade pursuers.

Customers from faraway places thronged to the Town Bakery every day to purchase its incomparable bread.

When a careless waiter spilled some greasy food on a patron's suit, the management hastily apologized and promised to pay the dry-cleaning bill.

Nobody in town could understand why Richard Cory, who seemed to have almost everything one could wish for, should have taken his own life.

Joe thought he might have trouble opening his new combination lock, but by following the accompanying instructions he was easily able to do so.

Some of the senators not reelected had incurred the wrath of many voters for opposing stricter pollution-control legislation.

QUESTIONS

11. Who led a tortuous chase? _____

12. Who alienated others? _____

13. Who declined a prerogative? _____

14. Who had explicit directions? _____

15. Who used provisional quarters? _____

16. Who was responsible for something that
    seemed bizarre? _____

17. Who made an irrevocable decision? _____

18. Who marketed a superlative product? _____

19. Who showed forbearance? _____

20. Who tried to mollify someone? _____

 BRAINTEASERS: Fill in the missing letters, as in 1, below.

---

1. Each side did its best not to __a_ _b_ _r_ _o_ **gate** the truce.

2. How can you go back on your word if you have given a
   sole __ __ promise?

3. The news is shocking; we are __ __ __ __ __ __ **aught**.

4. The din was so __ __ **support** __ __ __ __ that everyone left.

5. Jonas Salk's vaccine conquered polio, an extremely
   __ __ **rule** __ __ disease.

6. Nobody doubts our delegate's __ __ **leg** __ __ __ __ __ to democratic principles.

7. Was his response premeditated or
   __ __ __ __ **tan** __ __ __ __?

8. They continue to hoard wealth; their avarice is
   __ __ **sat** __ __ __ __ __.

9. When our candidate won, there was __ __ __ **demon** __ __ __
   at our headquarters.

10. Please refrain from making remarks that are not **germ** _ _ _ to our topic.

11. Slippery roads this morning triggered a(n) _ **ash** of minor accidents.

12. Two hours is a(n) _ _ _ _ **din** _ _ _ time to have to wait for a bus.

13. Before appearing in public, make sure you are **present** _ _ _ _.

14. Passengers had to don life jackets and _ _ _ _ _ _ **ate** the ship.

15. We value the enthusiastic support of our _ _ **den** _ fans.

16. Standing beside the six-footer was a **dim** _ _ _ _ _ _ _ toddler.

17. You won't have to bear the **on** _ _ of cleaning up alone; we'll all pitch in.

18. I ate the whole salad, except for one _ _ **red** of lettuce.

19. The news was unbelievably good; we were _ _ _ _ _ **ant**.

20. All of the mountain, except the **pin** _ _ _ _ _ _, was visible from the base.

LESSON 6

LESSON WORDS 1–10: Pronounce the word, spell it, study its meanings, and finish the sentence that follows it.

atypical (*adj.*)   not conforming to type; not typical; **irregular**;
ā-'tip-i-kəl   **unusual; abnormal**

1. It was an *atypical* summer day; we were (sweltering, shivering) ————————.

awe (*v.*)   inspire with *awe* (fear mixed with dread, wonder, or
'ȯ   veneration); **frighten; terrify**

2. Bathers relaxing on the beach were *awed* when they saw a (mountainous, gentle) ———————————— wave rolling in from the sea.

curt (*adj.*)   rudely brief; **abrupt; brusque**
'kərt

3. The workers were (pleased, offended) ———————— by the manager's *curt* replies to their questions.

domestic (*adj.*)   pertaining to one's own country or to a particular
də-'mes-tik   country; **national; internal**

4. A President overly concerned with events (at home, abroad) ———————— is likely to give inadequate attention to *domestic* problems.

duress (*n.*)   compulsion by threat; **coercion; constraint**
d(y)u̇-'res

5. The aide was under *duress* because he had recently been (reprimanded, complimented) ————————————.

formidable (*adj.*) tending to inspire awe or wonder by reason of
'fȯr-məd-ə-bəl   notable size, power, superiority, or excellence;
superior; **outstanding**

6. In comparison with an (ant, elephant) _____,
a human being is of *formidable* proportions.

friction (*n.*) clashing between two persons or parties of opposed
'frik-shən   views; **conflict**; **dissension**; **disagreement**

7. Last year, there was *friction* between the neighbors, but

now they seem to (like, distrust) _____
each other.

identical (*adj.*) similar or alike in every way; **equal**; **equivalent**
ī-'dent-i-kəl

8. If prices here are *identical* with those charged in all the

other shops in town, there is (no, good) _____
reason to suspect price fixing.

indubitable (*adj.*) too evident to be doubted; **unquestionable**;
in-'d(y)ü-bət-ə-bəl   **indisputable**

9. Statements from (authoritative, unofficial) _____
sources usually cannot be regarded as *indubitable*.

inequity (*n.*) lack of fairness; **injustice**; **wrong**
in-'ek-wət-ē

10. It was an *inequity* for those who worked overtime to be

paid (the same as, more than) _____ those
who did not.

SENTENCE COMPLETION 1–10: Enter the required lesson
words.

---

1. A confession that may have been made under _____

is not _____ evidence of a suspect's guilt.

2. Our two senators tend to agree on what our foreign policy should be, but there is sometimes _____ between them on _____ issues.

3. The _____ refusal of one person to contribute to the community fund was _____; everyone else we approached was glad to make a donation.

4. Most of the contestants were not eager for a match with the _____ champion because they were _____ **d** by her reputation.

5. This company believes that there should be no _____ in pay for men and women who do _____ work.

 SYNONYM ROUNDUP 1–10: Each line, when completed, should have three synonyms. Enter the missing letters.

---

1. inj __ st __ ce   wr __ ng   __ __ equity

2. abr __ pt   c __ rt   br __ sque

3. c __ nfl __ ct   fr __ ction   dis __ __ nsion

4. un __ s __ al   __ __ regular   __ typical

5. eq __ __ l   id __ nt __ cal   __ quival __ nt

6. __ we   fri __ __ ten   terr __ fy

7. int __ rn __ l   n __ tion __ l   d __ m __ stic

8. __ __ question __ ble   indisp __ t __ ble   ind __ bit __ ble

9. constr __ __ nt   d __ ress   c __ __ rcion

10. s __ p __ rior   form __ d __ ble   __ __ __ standing

LESSON WORDS 11–20: Pronounce the word, spell it, study its meanings, and finish the sentence that follows it.

---

legitimate (*adj.*)   in accordance with the law; **legal**; **lawful**; **gen-**
li-ˈjit-ə-mət   **uine**

    11. If (the Treasury, counterfeiters) _____ printed this $100 bill, it is not *legitimate*.

perpetrator (*n.*)   one who *perpetrates* (commits) a crime or of-
ˈpər-pə-ˌtrāt-ər   fense; **criminal**; **culprit**

    12. Society is less secure when *perpetrators* are (behind bars, at large) _____ .

premature (*adj.*)   occurring or done before the proper time;
ˌprē-mə-ˈchu̇(ə)r   **early**; **untimely**

    13. A snowfall in Chicago in (August, January) _____ would be *premature*.

specify (*v.*)   make something specific; **stipulate**; **detail**
ˈspes-ə-ˌfī

    14. To (incur, avoid) _____ heavy fines, the property owners must make the repairs that the court order *specifies*.

stymie (*v.*)   stand in the way of; **block**; **thwart**; **hinder**
ˈstī-mē

    15. Many immigrants manage to succeed; (knowledge, ignorance) _____ of their new country's language does not seem to *stymie* them.

tally (*v.*)   make a count of; **add**; **total**
ˈtal-ē

    16. To *tally* long columns of figures without a calculator, one must be proficient in (multiplication, addition) _____ .

unremitting (*adj.*) not slackening or abating; **constant; inces-**
ˌən-ri-ˈmit-iŋ   **sant; unabated**

17. Serious consequences may ensue if infants learning to
    (talk, walk) _____ do not receive *unremitting* sur-
    veillance.

utter (*adj.*) carried to the utmost point or highest degree; **com-**
ˈət-ər   **plete; absolute**

18. Things were (under, beyond) _____ control;
    there was *utter* chaos.

vociferous (*adj.*) vehement or noisy in making one's feelings
vō-ˈsif-ə-rəs   known; **clamorous; vocal**

19. It would be atypical for our *vociferous* friends to be (si-
    lent, articulate) _____ when controver-
    sial issues are discussed.

wake (*n.*) visible turbulence or path left by a moving body; **trail;**
ˈwāk   **track**

20. In clear weather, passengers looking in the direction that
    the ship is (going, leaving) _____ can see its
    wake.

SENTENCE COMPLETION 11–20: Enter the required lesson words from D, above.

1. Any claim of victory by either side would be _____

   at this time because we have not yet begun to _____

   the votes.

2. Promotions are in line for the officers whose _____

   efforts led to the apprehension of the _____s.

3. The lease _____ **s** the services tenants are to receive; if such services are not delivered, there are _____ grounds for complaint.

4. The proposal to build a garbage disposal plant in this community is being _____ **d** by _____ protests from the residents.

5. When a tornado hits an area, it leaves _____ destruction in its _____ .

 SYNONYM ROUNDUP 11–20: Each line, when completed, should have three words similar in meaning. Enter the missing letters.

---

11. compl __ te	abs __ l __ te	__ tter
12. __ __ wart	st __ mie	__ lock
13. tr __ ck	__ __ ail	w __ ke
14. spec __ fy	st __ p __ late	d __ tail
15. p __ rp __ trat __ r	c __ lpr __ t	cr __ m __ nal
16. t __ t __ l	__ dd	__ ally
17. e __ rly	__ __ timely	__ __ __ mature
18. v __ cal	v __ c __ f __ rous	cl __ m __ rous
19. leg __ l	leg __ t __ m __ te	gen __ __ ne
20. const __ nt	__ __ remitting	inc __ ss __ nt

 SYNONYMS: To avoid repetition, replace the boldfaced word with a synonym from the vocabulary list below.

---

absolute   equivalent   detail   frighten   unabated
injustice   premature   count   culprit   unusual

1. There is no remission in the storm; it continues to rage with **unremitting** fury.

1. _____

2. Isn't it inequitable for one player to get the lion's share of the credit? How do you think the rest of the team feels about this **inequity**?

2. _____

3. On a typical day, there are long delays on the roads in the rush hour, but today was **atypical**; traffic was light.

3. _____

4. The railroad's timetable gives valuable specific information; it **specifies** the time of arrival and departure of each train.

4. _____ **s**

5. Keep Andy out of the dining room until the right time; his **untimely** entry could spoil the surprise we have planned for his birthday.

5. _____

6. We were utterly fascinated by the show; it was an **utter** delight.

6. _____

7. Are there still some untallied ballots to be **tallied**?

7. _____ **ed**

8. Most residents were **awed** when they heard the awesome consequences that might ensue if they did not evacuate the area.

8. _____ **ed**

9. A considerable time elapsed between the perpetration of the deception and the arrest of the **perpetrator**.

9. _____

10. Since the three cameras have **identical** features, once we find out what each one costs, we can identify the best buy.

10. _____

> **H** **ANTONYMS:** In the blank space in each sentence below, enter the word most nearly the antonym of the boldfaced word or expression. Choose your antonyms from the following list.

abating	**questionable**	**late**	**stymie**	**foreign**
equality	**courteous**	**harmony**	**unlawful**	**stipulate**

1. A drop in the output of **domestic** oil refineries requires us to increase our imports of _____ oil.

2. _____ exactly how you want your food to be cooked; don't blame the restaurant if you **fail to specify** your requirements.

3. The _____ we had hoped for was never realized; we had nothing but **friction**.

4. The Count of Monte Cristo always arrived exactly on time for an appointment; he was never **premature** or _____.

5. The pain, fiercely **unremitting** at first, is gradually _____.

6. The accused company insists that all of its business is **legitimate**; it denies any involvement in _____ operations.

7. _____ of opportunity for all citizens is the goal of democracy; it is pledged to eradicate **inequity**.

8. A judge's honesty must be **indubitable**; anyone whose truthfulness is _____ should not sit on the bench.

9. Your **curt** refusal of their offer to help you is unlikely to win you any friends. Couldn't you have responded in a more _____ way?

10. Others did not **thwart** his ambitions; it was his own lack of perseverance that _____**d** him.

CONCISE WRITING: Express the thought of each sentence in NO MORE THAN FOUR WORDS.

1. Some of the individuals who have committed crimes show a deep and painful regret for what they have done.

   _____

2. The conclusions that you and I have reached seem alike in every way.

   _____

3. Many a time, clashes between persons or parties of opposing views stand in the way of progress.

   _____

4. The talent that she possesses is too obvious to be doubted.

   _____

5. Storms that are accompanied by lightning and loud claps of thunder inspire people with a kind of fear that is mixed with dread, wonder, or veneration.

   _____

ANALOGIES: Which lettered pair of words—**a, b, c, d,** or **e**—most nearly has the same relationship as the numbered pair? Enter the letter of your answer in the space provided.

1. LEGITIMATE : FORBID

   a. permissible : allow   *b.* insignificant : overlook
   c. intelligible : comprehend *d.* accessible : reach
   e. irrevocable : undo   1. _____

2. ATYPICAL : NORMAL

   a. ardent : enthusiastic   *b.* provisional : makeshift
   c. ambiguous : clear   *d.* fortuitous : casual
   e. fickle : capricious   2. _____

3. UNREMITTING : SLACKEN

   a. persistent : persevere
   c. grateful : appreciate
   e. jubilant : rejoice

   b. indefatigable : tire
   d. penitent : regret

   3. _____

4. FORMIDABLE : RESPECT

   a. despicable : contempt
   c. inane : repetition
   e. meritorious : censure

   b. mediocre : admiration
   d. irreparable : repair

   4. _____

5. TELLER : TALLY

   a. meddler : expedite
   c. glutton : fast
   e. tightwad : squander

   b. narrator : recount
   d. shirker : work

   5. _____

6. CURT : BREVITY

   a. futile : effectiveness
   c. mendacious : truth
   e. impeccable : perfection

   b. irrelevant : pertinence
   d. spontaneous : premeditation

   6. _____

7. VOCIFEROUS : DIN

   a. impartial : resentment
   c. vague : doubt
   e. incompetent : confidence

   b. flexible : stalemate
   d. imperturbable : panic

   7. _____

8. SPECIFY : EXPLICIT

   a. simplify : difficult
   c. withhold : available
   e. curtail : lengthy

   b. underline : emphatic
   d. clarify : obscure

   8. _____

9. SHIP : WAKE

   a. eagle : beak
   c. train : track
   e. navigator : course

   b. skunk : odor
   d. bloodhound : scent

   9. _____

10. INEQUITY : REDRESS

   a. rumor : believe
   c. debt : repay
   e. promise : break

   b. problem : ignore
   d. bribe : offer

   10. _____

LESSON 7

LESSON WORDS 1–10: Pronounce the word, spell it, study its meanings, and finish the sentence that follows it.

apathy (*n.*) lack of feeling, concern, or interest; **coolness**; **in-**
'ap-ə-thē   **difference**

1. The (high, low) _____ percentage of the elector-
ate that stayed away from the polls on Election Day is
probably a sign of voter *apathy.*

appall (*v.*) fill with horror or dismay; **shock**; **horrify**
ə-'pȯl

2. We are *appalled* by the large number of drivers (observing, exceeding) _____ the speed limit.

asset (*n.*) anything owned that has exchange value or is benefi-
'as-ˌet   cial; **resource**; **advantage** (Note: the plural **assets**
means *wealth.*)

3. Every dollar you (squander, save) _____
diminishes your *assets.*

cardinal (*adj.*) of principal importance; **chief**; **main**; **primary**
'kärd-ᵊn-əl

4. I forgot the (trivial, important) _____ as-
pects of the address but remembered its *cardinal* point.

exclusive (*adj.*) excluding all others from participation; **whole**;
iks-'klü-siv   **undivided**; **sole**

5. As long as Keith has *exclusive* use of the camera, (everyone, nobody) _____ else can take pictures
with it.

fiasco (*n.*)   complete or ridiculous failure; **flop**; **disaster**
fē-'as-kō

> 6. The (presence, absence) _____ of the guest
>   of honor turned the lavishly prepared reception into a *fi-
>   asco*.

fractious (*adj.*)   hard to manage; **refractory**; **unruly**
'frak-shəs

> 7. There is (strong, little) _____ likelihood of a
>   harmonious public hearing if the audience is in a *fractious*
>   mood.

gusto (*n.*)   hearty or keen enjoyment; **relish**; **zest**
'gəs-tō

> 8. They must have been (bored, fascinated) _____
>   by the game because they entered into it with *gusto*.

incapacitate (*v.*)   make incapable or unfit; **disable**; **paralyze**;
ˌin-kə-'pas-ə-ˌtāt   **disqualify**

> 9. Those who are temporarily *incapacitated* cannot (work,
>   recover) _____ .

invincible (*adj.*)   incapable of being conquered, defeated, or sub-
(')in-'vin-sə-bəl   dued; **insuperable**; **indomitable**

> 10. After a dozen (losses, victories) _____
>   in a row, we thought we were *invincible*.

SENTENCE COMPLETION 1–10: Enter the required lesson
words.

---

1. The   expensive   Maginot   Line,   built   to   make   France

   _____ , was a(n) _____ be-

   cause it failed to prevent a German invasion.

2. We were _____**ed** to learn that some home-

owners have been disregarding a(n) _____

safety regulation—they have not installed smoke alarms.

3. It was hard to overcome Jane's _____ for exercise,

but when she saw what it was doing for her friends she began

to participate with _____.

4. The high-salaried athlete who was _____**d**

by a leg injury in the opening game was no _____

to the team for the rest of the season.

5. One _____ child received the almost _____

attention of the instructor to the detriment of the rest of the

group.

 SYNONYM ROUNDUP 1–10: Each line, when completed, should have three synonyms. Enter the missing letters.

---

1. pr __ mary   c __ rd __ nal   ch __ __ f

2. horr __ fy   sh __ ck   __ __ pall

3. advant __ ge   res __ __ rce   ass __ t

4. z __ st   r __ lish   g __ sto

5. __ __ capac __ tate   __ __ __ able   paral __ ze

6. wh __ le   __ __ divided   excl __ s __ ve

7. invinc __ ble   ins __ per __ ble   ind __ mit __ ble

8. dis __ ster   fl __ p   f __ asco

9. c __ __ lness   __ pathy   __ __ difference

10. unr __ ly   fr __ ctious   refr __ ct __ ry

 LESSON WORDS 11–20: Pronounce the word, spell it, study its meanings, and finish the sentence that follows it.

---

obsess (*v.*) excessively preoccupy the thoughts of; **haunt**; be-
äb-ˈses   **set**; **trouble**

11. A (vindictive, forgiving) _____ person is *obsessed* with a desire for revenge.

pernicious (*adj.*) highly injurious or destructive; **ruinous**;
pər-ˈnish-əs   **deadly**; **hurtful**

12. Addiction to the use of *pernicious* substances can (en-
hance, undermine) _____ a person's
well-being.

perverse (*adj.*) willfully determined not to do what is right, rea-
(ˌ)pər-ˈvərs   sonable, or accepted; **contrary**; **wrongheaded**

13. It is *perverse* to pursue a course of action that is (self-
fulfilling, self-destructive) _____.

qualm (*n.*) feeling of uneasiness, especially about a point of con-
ˈkwäm   science or propriety; **scruple**; **compunction**

14. An employee who is not really (ill, well) _____
should have no *qualm* about staying home from work.

raze (*v.*) level to the ground; tear down; **demolish**; **destroy**
ˈrāz

15. All structures (outside, in) _____ the proposed
path of the new expressway will be *razed*.

resourceful (*adj.*)   able to meet situations promptly and skillfully;
ri-'zórs-fəl   capable of devising ways and means; **quick-witted**; **intelligent**

16. When he could not support his family by selling rugs, the *resourceful* merchant went (out of, into another) _____ business.

selfless (*adj.*)   devoted to others' welfare or interests rather than
'sel-fləs   one's own; **unselfish**; **altruistic**

17. A (benefactor, swindler) _____ does not have *selfless* motives.

stupefy (*v.*)   overwhelm with amazement; **astound**; **astonish**
'stü-pə-ˌfī

18. Because of the (mass, lack) _____ of evidence against the suspect, many were *stupefied* when they heard the jury's verdict of acquittal.

taint (*v.*)   modify by, or as if by, a trace of something offensive;
'tānt   **corrupt**; **contaminate**

19. The candidate's rivals are suggesting that he may have been *tainted* by his acquaintance with a former (swindler, mediator) _____ .

unqualified (*adj.*)   without *qualification* (restriction); **unre-**
ˌən-'kwäl-ə-ˌfīd   **stricted**; **complete**

20. (Lukewarm, Devoted) _____ friends can usually be counted on for *unqualified* support.

SENTENCE COMPLETION 11–20: Enter the required lesson words from D, above.

---

1. In the years they were addicted to the _____

   habit of smoking, their hair, breath, and garments were

   _____**ed** with the smell of tobacco.

2. We were _____ **ed** to find the highway closed for no apparent reason, but our _____ driver took us to our destination by an alternate route.

3. The _____ refusal of one resident to move to more comfortable quarters has stymied plans to _____ the dilapidated six-story apartment building.

4. The candidate's _____ service to our community entitles her to our _____ endorsement.

5. The new passengers were _____ **ed** by fears that the boat might turn over, but the regulars had no _____ **s** about its seaworthiness.

F   **SYNONYM ROUNDUP 11–20:** Enter the missing letters.

---

11. __ __ selfish   __ __ __ __ less   altr __ istic

12. dem __ lish   __ __ stroy   r __ ze

13. h __ __ nt   tr __ __ ble   __ __ sess

14. ast __ nish   st __ p __ fy   ast __ __ nd

15. contr __ ry   perv __ rse   wrongh __ __ ded

16. unqu __ l __ fied   __ __ restricted   c __ mplete

17. intell __ gent   r __ sourceful   __ __ ick-witted

18. contam __ nate   t __ __ nt   c __ rr __ pt

19. d __ __ __ dly   ru __ nous   pernic __ ous

20. qu __ lm   scr __ ple   c __ mp __ nction

SYNONYMS: To avoid repetition, replace the boldfaced word with a synonym from the vocabulary list below.

---

unrestricted	indifference
altruistic	horrify
wrongheaded	unruly
sole	resourceful
astound	trouble

1. Dolores must think she has **exclusive** rights to the telephone; she has to be continually reminded that it is not exclusively hers.

   1. _____

2. The chief stumbling block in the fight against pollution has been our **apathy**; we can no longer afford to be apathetic.

   2. _____

3. The singer was absolutely **stupefied** by the public response to his new album; it has been a stupefying success.

   3. _____**ed**

4. Her **perverse** determination not to see a physician was unfortunate; if not for that perversity she would have recovered much sooner.

   4. _____

5. We are **appalled** by the length of the strike; both union and management are showing an appalling lack of concern for the public welfare.

   5. _____**ed**

6. In an emergency, we must have all our wits about us; if we are not **quick-witted**, we may not survive.

6. _____

7. Your learner's permit is not an **unqualified** license to drive. One qualification, for example, is that a licensed driver must accompany you when you drive.

7. _____

8. Disregarding the danger to herself, she rushed to the aid of the victim; she was utterly **selfless**.

8. _____

9. For a time, he was **obsessed** by the fear of losing his job, but fortunately that is no longer an obsession.

9. _____**d**

10. If the police were not on hand to restrain the **fractious** crowd, there might have been some serious infractions of the law.

10. _____

ANTONYMS: In the blank space in each sentence below, enter the word most nearly the antonym of the boldfaced word. Choose your antonyms from the following list.

enthusiasm	**orderly**	**liability**	**loathing**	**decontaminate**
beatable	**build**	**harmless**	**hit**	**nonessential**

1. The flood victims had anticipated going home with **gusto**, but once there, the chore of having to clean up all the mud filled them with _____.

2. Rain, in normal amounts, is an **asset** at planting time, but too much of it can be a serious _____.

3. The construction company will **raze** the existing structure and

   _____ a replacement for it on the same site.

4. The child soon develops an **apathy** for most of her new toys,

   but she still has _____ for her old rag doll.

5. The show almost everyone thought would be a(n) _____
   proved to be a **fiasco**.

6. Because its top scorer is sidelined with injuries, the up-to-now

   invincible team seems to be _____.

7. The club had a relatively _____ meeting yester-
   day because its most **fractious** member happened to be ab-
   sent.

8. Some of the things I took along for the beach were really

   _____, but I forgot one **cardinal**
   item—my towel.

9. Drinking water from the sources **tainted** by the accidental

   chemical spill will have to be _____ **d**
   before it can be safely used.

10. Substances like tobacco and asbestos, formerly considered

    _____, were widely used before their **perni-
    cious** nature was discovered.

 CONCISE WRITING: Make the following passages more concise, using no more than the number of words suggested.

---

1. The lack of feeling and concern that they are showing is hard to
   believe, especially at this time, when we are engaged in a struggle to get ourselves out of a difficult and entrapping situation
   that we have fallen into.   (*Cut to about 15–20 words*.)

   _____

   _____

2. The negotiations will be a ridiculous failure if one side or the other remains willfully determined not to do what is right or reasonable.   (*Cut to about 10–12 words*.)

_____

_____

3. Wilbert is so devoted to the welfare and interests of others, rather than his own, and so able to meet situations promptly and skillfully, that we have no feeling of uneasiness about giving him our complete and undivided backing.   (*Cut to about 16–18 words*.)

_____

_____

4. We were overcome with amazement when we heard that the building that we have been living in will soon be leveled to the ground.   (*Cut to about 11–13 words*.)

_____

_____

5. What makes you think that the family car is your personal property, and that no one else has a right to use it? Your attitude fills us with dismay.   (*Cut to about 15–18 words*.)

_____

_____

6. The manager's thoughts are preoccupied to an excessive degree with a suspicion that those who don't like him are making up highly injurious rumors about him.   (*Cut to about 15–18 words*.)

_____

_____

ANALOGIES: Which lettered pair of words—**a, b, c, d,** or **e**—most nearly has the same relationship as the numbered pair? Enter the letter of your answer in the space provided.

1. STUPEFY : AMAZEMENT

    a. humiliate : pride
    c. nettle : composure
    e. infuriate : rage

    b. exonerate : blame
    d. interrogate : information

    1. _____

2. ALTRUIST : SELFLESS

    a. worrywart : optimistic
    c. braggart : humble
    e. nonconformist : compliant

    b. extremist : moderate
    d. loyalist : staunch

    2. _____

3. RAZE : CONSTRUCT

    a. taint : decontaminate
    c. diminish : abate
    e. provoke : foment

    b. fume : bristle
    d. tarnish : soil

    3. _____

4. APATHETIC : INTEREST

    a. resourceful : means
    c. well-intentioned : malice
    e. enthusiastic : gusto

    b. garrulous : chatter
    d. penitent : regret

    4. _____

    Hint: An APATHETIC person lacks INTEREST.

5. INCAPACITATE : INCAPABLE

    a. disparage : friendly
    c. mollify : dissatisfied
    e. perturb : calm

    b. malign : grateful
    d. encourage : sanguine

    5. _____

6. ASSET : ADVANTAGE

    a. grievance : pleasure
    c. accident : caution
    e. possibility : certainty

    b. problem : thorn
    d. blessing : curse

    6. _____

7. CRIME : APPALL

    a. drudgery : bore   *b.* conflict : resolve

    c. misinformation : enlighten   *d.* defect : repair

    e. reversal : gratify   7. _____

8. SPOILSPORT : PERVERSE

    a. gossip : discreet   *b.* peer : inferior

    c. loafer : industrious   *d.* bungler : meticulous

    e. oaf : gullible   8. _____

9. FIASCO : MORTIFICATION

    a. indolence : progress   *b.* glut : overproduction

    c. wound : pain   *d.* undernourishment : food

    e. despair : hope   9. _____

    Hint: A FIASCO causes MORTIFICATION.

10. CLIQUE : EXCLUSIVE

    a. assortment : identical   *b.* mob : manageable

    c. sanctuary : unsafe   *d.* onus : burdensome

    e. fabrication : true   10. _____

LESSON 8

LESSON WORDS 1–10: Pronounce the word, spell it, study its meanings, and finish the sentence that follows it.

---

alleged (*adj.*)   accused but not proven or convicted; **suspected**;
ə-'lejd   **supposed**

1. In an American court, an *alleged* perpetrator is considered
(guilty, innocent) _____ before testimony
begins.

asinine (*adj.*)   marked by inexcusable failure to exercise intelli-
'as-ᵊn-ˌīn   gence or sound judgment; **stupid**; **inane**; **fatu-
ous**; **silly**

2. Moira gives (scant, careful) _____ attention
to Sam's ideas because she considers them *asinine*.

cursory (*adj.*)   done rapidly, without attention to details; **hasty**;
'kərs-ə-rē   **superficial**

3. A *cursory* reading of a biography usually yields a (thor-
ough, limited) _____ understanding of its importance.

defection (*n.*)   conscious abandonment of allegiance or duty; **de-
di-'fek-shən   sertion**; **apostasy**

4. The prime minister's influence has been (augmented, pared)
_____ by the *defection* of a bloc of her supporters.

delude (*v.*)   mislead the mind or judgment of; **deceive**; **trick**;
di-'lüd   **fool**

5. Don Quixote *deluded* himself into thinking that the wind-
mills he saw were (energy producers, evil giants)
_____ .

70

diagnose (*v.*)   make a *diagnosis* (investigation into the cause or
'dī-ig-ˌnōs   nature of a condition, situation, or problem); **iden-
                     tify**; **recognize**

6. With (insufficient, adequate) _____
   medical evidence, a physician cannot *diagnose* a patient's
   illness.

dramatic (*adj.*)   highly effective; **striking**; **startling**; **sensa-
drə-'mat-ik   tional**

7. I cannot (recall, forget) _____ the exact words
   the keynote speaker said because they were so *dramatic*.

expunge (*v.*)   strike or blot out; **erase**; **obliterate**
ik-'spənj

8. It is (more, less) _____ difficult to judge the financial condition of a company if crucial transactions have been
   expunged from its records.

inestimable (*adj.*)   too great or valuable to be estimated; **incal-
in-'es-tə-mə-bəl   culable**; **immeasurable**

9. Ordinarily, people are (eager, reluctant) _____
   to part with something of *inestimable* worth.

inventory (*n.*)   quantity of goods on hand; **stock**; **supply**
'in-vən-ˌtȯr-ē

10. Merchants whose *inventory* is low may soon have (over-
    stocked, bare) _____ shelves.

SENTENCE COMPLETION 1–10: Enter the required lesson
words.

---

1. It is _____—because you have won the spelling

bee—to _____ yourself into thinking you are infal-

lible.

2. The _____ of Benedict Arnold, a brave general who had given _____ service to his country, came as a shocking surprise.

3. When the hasty reprimand of the officer for _____
   incompetence was reviewed, it was declared unwarranted and
   _____**d** from his record.

4. The _____ rise in sales means that retailers
   will have to hurry to replenish their _____**ies**.

5. Our mechanic needs more time to _____ the
   problem with our car; a(n) _____ check under
   the hood did not show what was wrong.

© **SYNONYM ROUNDUP 1–10:** Each line, when completed, should have three synonyms. Enter the missing letters.

---

1. dec __ __ ve   tr __ ck   del __ de

2. st __ rtling   d __ __ matic   str __ king

3. in __ ne   fat __ ous   as __ nine

4. st __ ck   s __ pply   invent __ __ __

5. all __ g __ d   s __ spected   supp __ sed

6. er __ se   obl __ t __ rate   exp __ nge

7. reco __ nize   d __ __ gnose   id __ __ tify

8. h __ sty   c __ rs __ ry   superfic __ __ l

9. incalc __ lable   __ __ measurable   in __ st __ m __ ble

10. des __ rtion   __ __ fection   aposta __ y

LESSON WORDS 11–20: Pronounce the word, spell it, study its meanings, and finish the sentence that follows it.

lamentable (*adj.*) to be regretted; **deplorable**; **unfortunate**
'lam-ən-tə-bəl

    11. Since the oversight had a (negligible, considerable)

    _____ effect on our morale, it was

    especially *lamentable.*

mandate (*n.*) authoritative command; **order**; **directive**
'man-ˌdāt

    12. No government official may lawfully (heed, ignore)

    _____ a constitutional *mandate.*

overhaul (*v.*) subject to strict examination with a view to correc-
ˌo-vər-'hȯl   tion or repair; restore to serviceable condition; **re-
    pair**; **recondition**

    13. Some (trouble-free, troublesome) _____
    engines often have to be *overhauled.*

paucity (*n.*) smallness of number or quantity; **fewness**; **dearth**;
'pȯ-sət-ē   **scarcity**

    14. When Mother Hubbard's cupboard was (full, bare)

    _____, there was no *paucity* of food.

perplex (*v.*) make (someone) uncertain, doubtful, or hesitant;
pər-'pleks   **puzzle**; **bewilder**

    15. I was *perplexed* by some of the (explicit, ambiguous)

    _____ statements in the manual.

rudimentary (*adj.*) having to do with the *rudiments* (first prin-
ˌrüd-ə-'ment-ə-rē   ciples) of a subject; **elementary**; **begin-
    ning**

    16. She has a *rudimentary* knowledge of scuba diving; she is

    a(n) (expert, novice) _____ in the sport.

scrupulous (*adj.*)   1. having moral integrity; **upright**; **honor-**
'skrü-pyə-ləs   **able**
                       2. extremely careful to do the precisely right,
                          proper, or correct thing in every last detail;
                          painstaking; **punctilious**

    17. We were *scrupulous* in our housecleaning; we vacuumed
        every accessible square inch of floor space, (except, even)

        _____ under the beds.

unprincipled (*adj.*)   lacking, or not based on, moral principles;
‚ən-'prin-sə-pəld   **unconscionable**; **corrupt**

    18. *Unprincipled*   vendors   (unintentionally,   knowingly)

        _____ overcharge customers.

vexatious (*adj.*)   causing irritation or annoyance; **distressing**;
vek-'sā-shəs   **troublesome**

    19. A *vexatious* problem is a (snap to solve, thorn in one's side)

    _____ .

victimize (*v.*)   make a victim of; subject to deception or fraud;
'vik-tə-‚mīz   **defraud**; **swindle**; **hoodwink**

    20. (Punishment, Compensation) _____
        has been set by court mandate for those who were *victim-*
        ized.

SENTENCE COMPLETION 11–20: Enter the required lesson words from D, above.

1. Students still _____ **ed** by _____

concepts in arithmetic are not quite ready for advanced mathe-

matics.

2. Despite the _____ problems confronting the

city, there is no _____ of candidates for the

mayoralty.

3. The new county executive believes her election by a landslide gives her a _____ to _____ the county's allegedly inefficient bureaus.

4. An undercover probe showed that some _____ mechanics had _____**d** car owners by billing them for repairs that were not made.

5. A more _____ check of the commencement program before it was printed would have prevented the _____ omission of one graduate's name.

 SYNONYM ROUNDUP 11–20: Enter the missing letters.

---

11. ord __ r   d __ rective   m __ nd __ te

12. p __ rplex   __ __ wilder   p __ zzle

13. tr __ __ blesome   d __ stressing   v __ x __ tious

14. l __ ment __ ble   depl __ rable   unfort __ nate

15. r __ pair   overh __ __ l   __ __ condition

16. h __ n __ r __ ble   __ __ right   scr __ p __ lous

17. sc __ rcity   p __ __ city   __ earth

18. defr __ __ d   v __ ct __ mize   h __ __ dwink

19. el __ m __ nt __ ry   begin __ __ ng   r __ d __ mentary

20. corr __ pt   __ __ principled   uncons __ __ onable

SYNONYMS: To avoid repetition, replace the boldfaced word with a synonym from the vocabulary list below.

suspected elementary
startling   inventory
bewilder   apostasy
deplorable hoodwink
identified   unconscionable

1. They have made victims of us once, but we are determined not to let them **victimize** us again.

1. _____

2. I have myself **diagnosed** my problem as a tendency to procrastinate, and no one who really knows me will dispute that diagnosis.

2. _____

3. One of the most **dramatic** moments in Shakespearean drama is Hamlet's conversation with the ghost of his murdered father.

3. _____

4. Some of the allegations against the **alleged** perpetrator may be difficult to prove in court.

4. _____

5. Instead of continuing to lament your **lamentable** experience, try to learn what caused it, so that you may prevent it from happening again.

5. _____

6. Those who already know the rudiments of swimming should not be getting the same **rudimentary** instruction as the non-swimmers.

6. _____

7. During the recent rash of snowstorms, many stores heavily stocked with snow shovels saw that **stock** diminish to zero.

8. The revolutionary movement, weakened by the **defection** of two key members, might have collapsed if any other members had defected.

9. The problems that **perplex** us today are in some ways more perplexing than those that confronted our ancestors.

10. Unfortunately, there are **unprincipled** competitors out to win by hook or crook, with utter disregard for moral principles.

7. _____

8. _____

9. _____

10. _____

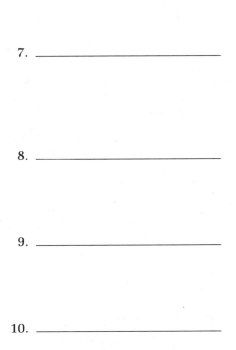

ANTONYMS: In the blank space in each sentence below, enter the word most nearly the antonym of the boldfaced word. Choose your antonyms from the following list.

worthless	**enlighten**	**fatuous**	**painstaking**	**abundance**
pleasant	**allegiance**	**remiss**	**undramatic**	**fortunate**

1. A **cursory** inspection will not do; this matter requires _____ scrutiny.

2. She said she had **startling** news, but the disclosure she made was quite _____.

3. Business was bad; merchants with a(n) _____ of goods kept complaining of the **paucity** of customers.

4. The employee charged with being _____ had recently been lauded for **scrupulous** attention to duty.

5. We had expected him to say something **sensible**, but his re-marks were quite _____.

6. On the whole, Napoleon had had a(n) _____ military career before his **lamentable** invasion of Russia.

7. It is regrettable when one has a **vexatious** encounter with a person with whom one has always had _____ dealings.

8. Macbeth hoped the witches he consulted would _____ him about his future; he did not expect them to **delude** him.

9. The lost necklace, thought to have been of **inestimable** value, was only a(n) _____ imitation.

10. The ruler was appalled to learn of the **defection** of an aide whose _____ he had never doubted.

 CONCISE WRITING: Express the thought of each sentence in NO MORE THAN FOUR WORDS.

---

1. This book deals with elementary principles, rather than ad-vanced concepts, and is intended for beginners.

_____

2. Inspections most of the time are done rapidly, without attention to details.

_____

3. The dentist who is now taking care of us is extremely careful to do the precisely right, proper, or correct thing in every last detail of his work.

_____

4. The quantity of goods that they have on hand is getting smaller and smaller.

_____

5. Some statements that were made showed an inexcusable failure on the part of those who made them to exercise intelligence or sound judgment.

_____

6. Education is being subjected to strict examination with a view to correcting its shortcomings.

_____

ANALOGIES: Which lettered pair of words—**a, b, c, d,** or **e**— most nearly has the same relationship as the numbered pair? Enter the letter of your answer in the space provided.

1. DUNCE : ASININE

   _a._ lion : timid   _b._ hermit : social
   _c._ crow : melodious   _d._ bee : indolent
   _e._ mule : stubborn   1. _____

2. MANDATE : DISREGARD

   _a._ vessel : overload   _b._ perpetrator : try
   _c._ favor : appreciate   _d._ inequity : rectify
   _e._ obligation : meet   2. _____

3. LAMENTABLE : SORROW

   _a._ atypical : pattern   _b._ indubitable : doubt
   _c._ appalling : dismay   _d._ pernicious : influence
   _e._ unprincipled : morality   3. _____

4. APOSTATE : DEFECT

   _a._ instructor : learn   _b._ purchaser : sell
   _c._ creditor : owe   _d._ refugee : flee
   _e._ beneficiary : donate   4. _____

5. DIAGNOSIS : INVESTIGATION

   _a._ flower : daffodil   _b._ fruit : apple
   _c._ base : mountain   _d._ nicotine : poison
   _e._ tree : branch   5. _____

6. PUNCTILIOUS : UNTIDINESS

   a. indulgent : forbearance   *b.* dictatorial : disobedience
   c. courageous : hardship   *d.* staunch : dependability
   e. adaptable : innovation   6. _____

   Hint: A PUNCTILIOUS person does not tolerate
   UNTIDINESS.

7. ALLEGED : PROVEN

   a. capricious : predictable   *b.* explicit : unambiguous
   c. raucous : strident   *d.* myriad : innumerable
   e. tortuous : serpentine   7. _____

8. PAUCITY : SCARCITY

   a. friction : harmony   *b.* certitude : conviction
   c. want : affluence   *d.* complicity : noninvolvement
   e. fact : falsification   8. _____

9. EXPUNGE : ERASURE

   a. specify : misunderstanding *b.* expedite : obstruction
   c. promise : commitment   *d.* exonerate : blame
   e. decontaminate : pollution   9. _____

   Hint: When we EXPUNGE something, we make
          an ERASURE.

10. DRAMATIC : ATTENTION

   a. inconspicuous : observation *b.* exemplary : admiration
   c. run-of-the-mill : excitement *d.* trite : novelty
   e. mediocre : emulation   10. _____

LESSON 9

LESSON WORDS 1–10: Pronounce the word, spell it, study its meanings, and finish the sentence that follows it.

---

abominate (*v.*) hate or loathe intensely; **abhor**; **execrate**
ə-'bäm-ə-ˌnāt

1. Dom *abominates* some foods that he once (disliked, relished) _____ .

affliction (*n.*) cause of persistent mental or bodily pain; great suffering; **trouble**; **tribulation**
ə-'flik-shən

2. Laura's (truancy, scholarship) _____ was an *affliction* to her mother.

animate (*adj.*) possessing life; **living**; **alive**
'an-ə-mət

3. There was nothing *animate* there, except some (dust, spiders) _____ .

chronic (*adj.*) marked by long duration or frequent recurrence; **habitual**; **inveterate**
'krän-ik

4. Bill (often, rarely) _____ raises objections; he is a *chronic* complainer.

exploit (*v.*) utilize selfishly for one's own ends; impose on; **abuse**; **use**
ik-'splȯit

5. Those receiving (higher, lower) _____ pay than others doing the same work felt they were being *exploited*.

fancy (*v.*) believe without being absolutely sure or certain; **imag-**
ˈfan-sē   **ine; think**

> 6. Until she heard the (jeers, cheers) _____ , the
> nervous singer *fancied* she had done poorly.

fell (*v.*) cause to fall; cut, break, or bring down; **prostrate**; **level**;
ˈfel   **down**

> 7. Her neighbors were (crestfallen, elated) _____
> when they saw that the storm had *felled* two of their fa-
> vorite trees.

gregarious (*adj.*) fond of the company of others; **sociable**; **so-**
gri-ˈge(ə)r-ē-əs   **cial**

> 8. Ordinarily, a *gregarious* person (loathes, enjoys)
> _____ going to a party.

innocuous (*adj.*) not harmful or injurious; unlikely to irritate;
in-ˈäk-yə-wəs   **harmless; inoffensive**

> 9. The prank was *innocuous*; there was no (harm, humor)
> _____ in it.

isolate (*v.*) set apart from others; **quarantine**; **segregate**
ˈi-sə-ˌlāt

> 10. It is not necessary to *isolate* a patient with a (communica-
> ble, noncommunicable) _____
> disease.

  SENTENCE COMPLETION 1–10: Enter the required lesson
words.

---

1. The statue looked so real that for a moment I _____**ed**

   it was _____ .

2. We _____ anyone who, for personal gain,

_____ **s** others.

3. The blow that might have _____ **ed** the champion

proved _____ because it was deflected.

4. Anyone suffering from a(n) _____ cold would

be grateful for a cure for this common _____ .

5. Being _____ , the troublemaker could not bear

to be _____ **d** from her companions, and she

promised to behave if permitted to rejoin them.

 SYNONYM ROUNDUP 1–10: Each line, when completed, should have three synonyms. Enter the missing letters.

---

1. im __ gine   th __ nk   f __ n __ y

2. al __ ve   an __ m __ te   l __ ving

3. ab __ se   __ se   expl __ __ t

4. s __ c __ able   soc __ __ l   gr __ g __ rious

5. tr __ __ ble   affl __ ction   tr __ b __ lation

6. h __ rmless   in __ __ cuous   __ __ offensive

7. pr __ str __ te   d __ __ n   __ ell

8. is __ late   __ __ gregate   qu __ r __ ntine

9. h __ b __ tual   chr __ nic   inv __ t __ rate

10. abh __ r   ab __ m __ nate   ex __ crate

LESSON WORDS 11–20: Pronounce the word, spell it, study its meanings, and finish the sentence that follows it.

---

positive (*adj.*) fully assured in an opinion or assertion; **confi-**
ˈpäz-ət-iv   **dent; sure; certain**

11. The police were *positive* they had the right suspect because he had left his (tools, fingerprints) _____
at the crime site.

precipitate (*v.*) hasten the occurrence of; bring about prema-
pri-ˈsip-ə-ˌtāt   turely; **speed; accelerate**

12. The (resumption, breakdown) _____ of
negotiations *precipitated* a crisis in the war-weary nation.

presumption (*n.*) assumption of something as true; **presup-**
pri-ˈzəm-shən   **position; premise**

13. Defendants tried in American courts are fortunate because their trial begins with a *presumption* of their (guilt,
innocence) _____ .

prior (*adj.*) earlier in time or order; **previous; preceding**
ˈprī-ər

14. Thank you for the invitation, but we made a *prior*
commitment to attend a wedding the day (of, before)
_____ your party.

propitious (*adj.*) tending to favor; **advantageous; favorable;**
prə-ˈpish-əs   **opportune**

15. Most shoppers regard (sale, ordinary) _____
days as a *propitious* time to buy.

redundant (*adj.*) exceeding what is necessary or normal; **super-**
ri-ˈdən-dənt   **fluous; excess**

16. With so (few, many) _____ cars remaining unsold
on the dealer's lot, another shipment from the factory at
this time would be *redundant*.

strategy (*n.*)   plan for achieving a desired result; **method**;
'strat-ə-jē   **scheme**

17. To put off training for an important tournament until just
before the first match is generally (good, poor) _____
strategy.

tentative (*adj.*)   offered or given for the time being; not final; sub-
'tent-ət-iv   ject to change; **conditional**; **provisional**

18. The company's decision to move is *tentative*; it (may yet,
will not) _____ be changed.

vanity (*n.*)   excessive pride in oneself or one's appearance; **con-
'van-ət-ē   ceit**; **egotism**; **self-admiration**

19. One obvious mark of *vanity* is a total (indifference to,
preoccupation with) _____
one's personal appearance.

veteran (*adj.*)   having had long practice in some occupation or
'vet-ə-rən   skill; **experienced**; **skilled**; **seasoned**

20. Automobile insurance rates tend to be much (lower,
higher) _____ for neophytes than for *veteran*
drivers.

SENTENCE COMPLETION 11–20: Enter the required lesson words from D, above.

---

1. If you hurt a vindictive person's _____ , you may

_____ some form of retaliation against you.

2. Since the plans for our trip are still _____ , we

cannot at this time be _____ about our dates

of departure and return.

3. We did not buy tickets in advance, on the _____

we could get them at the box office; but our _____

backfired—they were sold out.

4. The senator, a(n) _____ politician, is waiting

for a(n) _____ time to announce his candi-

dacy for the Presidency.

5. When asked to say something, I replied that _____

speakers had covered the topic so thoroughly that anything I

might say would be _____.

 SYNONYM ROUNDUP 11–20: Enter the missing letters.

11. sk __ lled	exper __ __ nced	v __ t __ ran
12. str __ t __ gy	sch __ me	meth __ d
13. __ __ rlier	pr __ v __ ous	pr __ __ __ r
14. cert __ __ n	s __ re	p __ s __ tive
15. fav __ r __ ble	pr __ pit __ ous	advantag __ __ us
16. self-adm __ r __ tion	v __ n __ ty	conc __ __ t
17. s __ perfl __ ous	ex __ ess	red __ nd __ nt
18. pr __ mise	__ __ __ sumption	pres __ pposition
19. __ __ celerate	sp __ __ d	pre __ ipitate
20. c __ nditional	pr __ visional	tent __ t __ ve

SYNONYMS: To avoid repetition, replace the boldfaced word with a synonym from the vocabulary list below.

scheme	**segregate**
living	**confident**
hasten	**presupposition**
tribulation	**egotism**
conditional	**abhor**

1. Were he to finish second, it would be a blow to his **vanity**; you know how vain he is.

1. _____

2. A common **affliction** that people complain of is rheumatism; millions are afflicted with it.

2. _____

3. I now realize that your apparent blunder was really a strategic move; it was the opening maneuver in your **strategy** for winning the game.

3. _____

4. **Animate** creatures are supposed to move with animation, so why not put some liveliness in your step?

4. _____

5. Presuming you would not be interested, they didn't discuss their trip with you, but they shouldn't have made that **presumption**.

5. _____

6. Most people **abominate** the weather we have been having; the potholes have been abominable.

6. _____

7. Management has made a **tentative** offer that the union has tentatively accepted.

7. _____

8. You cannot be **positive** they are wrong unless you are positively sure of the facts involved.

8. _____

9. I had **isolated** myself in a corner when a friendly group of four invited me to join them at their table; that ended my isolation.

9. _____**d**

10. Something we said must have **precipitated** their departure because they left precipitately, without saying goodbye.

10. _____**ed**

 ANTONYMS: In the blank space in each sentence below, enter the word most nearly the antonym of the boldfaced word. Choose your antonyms from the following list.

---

uncertain	**enjoy**	**link**	**inexperienced**	**subsequent**
asocial	**solace**	**final**	**pernicious**	**unfavorable**

1. DDT, a supposedly **innocuous** pesticide, was eventually discovered to have horribly _____ consequences.

2. Some people _____ living on a farm; others **abominate** it.

3. After being victimized by those he had trusted most, Silas Marner abandoned his **gregarious** lifestyle and became

_____ .

4. Communities **isolated** by the recent storm will be

_____**ed** again to the mainland once the bridge is repaired.

5. I thought I would be facing a **veteran** competitor in today's match, but he proved to be almost as _____ as I.

6. This seemed like a **propitious** day for our outing until an hour ago, when the weather turned _____ .

7. The parents had expected their child to be a(n) _____ to them in their old age, instead of an **affliction**.

8. Our mail is usually delivered a few minutes **prior** or _____ to lunch.

9. The president is **positive** that our organization does not have to raise its dues, but the treasurer is _____ that this is so.

10. At the moment, we have a **tentative** agreement, not a(n) _____ one.

 CONCISE WRITING: Express the thought of each sentence in NO MORE THAN FOUR WORDS.

---

1. Beware of excessive pride in yourself or in your personal appearance.

_____

2. This arrangement is for the time being only and is subject to change.

_____

3. They have a recurring and habitual inclination to put off what has to be done to some indefinite time in the future.

_____

4. He believes himself handsome without being absolutely sure or certain that he really is.

_____

5. Hurricanes cause so many trees to fall that it is impossible to count them.

_____

6. She has an intense loathing for those who utilize others for their own selfish ends.

_____

ANALOGIES: Which lettered pair of words—**a, b, c, d,** or **e**— most nearly has the same relationship as the numbered pair? Enter the letter of your answer in the space provided.

1. ATHLETE'S FOOT : AFFLICTION

    a. bird : worm   *b.* beverage : milk
    c. tree : cherry   *d.* rose : thorn
    e. vanity : foible   1. _____

2. REDUNDANT : GLUT

    a. noncontroversial : argument   *b.* inflammatory : riot
    c. mendacious : truth   *d.* capricious : reliability
    e. discreet : secret   2. _____

3. FELL : PROSTRATE

    a. abominate : hate   *b.* convict : absolve
    c. retrieve : lose   *d.* accelerate : retard
    e. grant : withhold   3. _____

4. INANIMATE : LIFE

    a. unfathomable : mystery   *b.* plausible : credibility
    c. consequential : importance   *d.* articulate : speech
    e. inane : sense   4. _____

5. GREGARIOUS : COMPANY

    a. scrupulous : untidiness   *b.* fractious : discipline
    c. voracious : eating   *d.* indolent : exertion
    e. apathetic : concern   5. _____

6. TENTATIVE : FINAL

    a. insignificant : meaningless   *b.* repetitious : concise
    c. fortuitous : accidental   *d.* bizarre : strange
    e. propitious : favorable   6. _____

7. INNOCUOUS : INJURY

    a. unwarranted : resentment   *b.* futile : purpose
    c. conspicuous : attention   *d.* explicit : ambiguity
    e. formidable : awe   7. _____

    Hint: Something INNOCUOUS does not cause
    INJURY.

8. VAIN : MODESTY

    a. malicious : ill will   *b.* diplomatic : tact
    c. vivacious : life   *d.* apprehensive : anxiety
    e. intrepid : timidity   8. _____

    Hint: A VAIN person lacks MODESTY.

9. EXPLOITER : SELFISH

    a. defector : loyal   *b.* fan : impartial
    c. altruist : selfless   *d.* optimist : panicky
    e. workaholic : lazy   9. _____

10. EGOTISTICAL : CONCEIT

    a. fatigued : exhaustion   *b.* late : opportunity
    c. feeble : assistance   *d.* fearful : confidence
    e. slow : progress   10. _____

LESSON 10: REVIEW AND ENRICHMENT

 CLOSE READING: Read the following statements. Then answer questions 1–10.

STATEMENTS

There was one vacant spot in the parking lot, but we couldn't take it because it was marked "Reserved for G.J. Smith."

On the merchant ship *Rights-of-Man*, Billy Budd was revered by almost everyone as a peacemaker.

During the Franco-Prussian War of 1870–71, the city of Paris was under siege for four and a half months before being compelled to surrender.

Despite a fortune spent by the promoters to publicize the concert, fewer than forty of the seats in the vast auditorium were occupied by curtain time.

The able and conscientious employee with whom we placed our order was in no way like the average salesperson one encounters in that store.

"Nonsense. Get back to work," said the supervisor, when a worker came up to complain of the lack of heat.

Of the three applicants, Chris had been a lifeguard, Pat had worked for the telephone company, and Sandy had never had a job.

With a leg in a cast and an arm in a sling, the hero of last week's game stood to acknowledge the ovation.

This mower was gone over by a specialist who straightened and sharpened the blade, replaced the spark plug, cleaned the filter, and tightened the bolts.

Before discarding the junk mail, Claudia glanced at some of the contents without going into depth.

QUESTIONS

1. Who engineered a fiasco? _____

2. Who was temporarily incapacitated? _____

3. Who overhauled something? _____

4. Who lacked prior occupational experience? _____

5. Who resolved friction? _____

6. Who was isolated from the rest of the world? _____

7. Who was atypical? _____

8. Who gave cursory attention to something? _____

9. Who had exclusive use of something? _____

10. Who was curt? _____

 CONCISE WRITING: Make the following passages more concise, using no more than the number of words suggested.

1. It is hard to believe that anyone could be so utterly lacking in moral principles as to make victims of people who are not able to help themselves.   (*Cut to about 15 words.*)

MODEL

It is incredible that anyone could be so unprincipled as to victimize helpless people.

2. Fred has long been in the habit of coming late to his appointments.   (*Cut to 5 words.*)

---

3. Smith is the one who is accused of perpetrating the crime, but who has not yet been convicted of it.   (*Cut to 5 words.*)

---

4. Do not let excessive pride in your achievements or your good looks mislead your mind or your judgment.   (*Cut to 5 words.*)

---

5. It is the highest degree of folly to be upset over a remark that Tamara made that obviously is unlikely to hurt or injure anyone.   (*Cut to about 12 words.*)

---

6. Her cousin has had years and years of experience in the art of mediating between sides that are opposed towards each other.   (*Cut to 6 words.*)

---

7. We believed, without being absolutely sure or certain, that someone was using us for selfish ends.   (*Cut to 6 words.*)

CLOSE READING: Read the following statements. Then answer questions 11–20.

STATEMENTS

Balboa gasped in wonder when, in 1513—from a lofty peak in Darien, in western Panama—he first caught sight of the vast Pacific.

Before opening her apparel shop, Darlene had taken a course in how to operate a small business.

The members were not thrilled with Cora's application for readmission, for she had abandoned the club in its early days when it was struggling to survive.

For a long time after the accident, the survivor was unable to think of anything else but that he was to blame for what had happened.

In taking the medication, Stephanie was extremely careful in observing her physician's instructions to the minutest detail.

The Serbian nationalist who assassinated an Austro-Hungarian archduke in Sarajevo, in 1914, provided the spark that ignited World War I.

Our representative was exceptionally vocal in opposing the proposal to close a firehouse in our neighborhood.

The colonial powers were generally opposed to granting autonomy to their colonies.

Julian remained loyal to the home team, though it had never won a pennant, and to those who belittled his idols, all he said was "Wait till next year."

Greg couldn't understand why the cheese had a soapy taste until he remembered that the checkout clerk had bagged the cheese with the soap.

QUESTIONS

11. Who studied the rudiments of something? _____

12. Who was a chronic optimist? _____

13. Who precipitated a global conflict? _____

14. Who was awed? _____

15. Who found that something had been tainted? _____

16. Who resented a defection? _____

17. Who was vociferous? _____

18. Who was obsessed? _____

19. Who exploited others? _____

20. Who was punctilious? _____

 BRAINTEASERS: Fill in the missing letters, as in 1, below.

---

1. Our health is a very precious **a s** set.

2. I was waiting for a **prop** _ _ _ _ _ _ moment to tell my joke.

3. Michelangelo taught his apprentices the _ _ **dime** _ _ _ of sculpture.

4. The fall shook up the athlete but did not

   _ _ **cap** _ _ _ _ _ _ _ her.

5. Like health, peace of mind is of _ **nest** _ _ _ _ _ _ value.

6. As **dome** _ _ _ _ reserves dwindle, our dependency on foreign sources grows.

7. The painting of the late duchess is so ___ ___ ___ **mate** that we feel her presence in the room.

8. A minor flaw, if not corrected, may become a

   vex ___ ___ ___ ___ ___ ___ problem.

9. The criminals operated a **leg** ___ ___ ___ ___ ___ ___ ___ business as a front for their illegal activities.

10. They didn't relish the cereal but devoured the cookies with

    ___ **us** ___ ___.

11. Centuries ago, oceans were **form** ___ ___ ___ ___ ___ ___ barriers to travelers.

12. The **card** ___ ___ ___ ___ objective of the United Nations is world peace.

13. We knew the Smiths, having met them on a(n) ___ ___ ___ **or** occasion.

14. The perpetrator had no ___ ___ **alms** about stealing from the poor.

15. A physician has to ___ ___ ___ ___ **nose** a patient's condition before treating it.

16. Stores with a huge ___ ___ **vent** ___ ___ ___ do not place large new orders with their suppliers.

17. The struggle for a more healthful environment must be

    ___ ___ ___ ___ **mitt** ___ ___ ___.

18. Your rejoicing is ___ ___ ___ **mature**; you haven't won anything yet.

19. The price of milk in all shops we visited was

    ___ **dent** ___ ___ ___ ___.

20. A ___ ___ **source** ___ ___ ___ person is good at devising ways to get things done.

LESSON 11

LESSON WORDS 1–10: Pronounce the word, spell it, study its meanings, and finish the sentence that follows it.

acrimonious (*adj.*) full of *acrimony* (harsh, biting sharpness in
ˌak-rə-ˈmō-nē-əs feeling, language, or manner); **caustic**;
stinging; **bitter**

  1. After their *acrimonious* exchange of words, it was difficult for the two to remain (friends, enemies)

  _____ .

amend (*v.*) alter formally by making modifications, additions, or
ə-ˈmend deletions; **change**; **rephrase**

  2. In 1920, the Constitution was *amended* to give women the
  right to vote, making the United States a (less, more)

  _____ democratic nation.

bias (*n.*) mental leaning, preference, or inclination; **one-sided-**
ˈbī-əs **ness**; **partiality**; **prejudice**

  3. To avoid possible charges of *bias*, a judge should not
  preside at the trial of a (friend, stranger)

  _____ .

cognizant (*adj.*) knowledgeable of something; **conscious**;
ˈkäg-nə-zənt **aware**; **mindful**

  4. Our surprise party for Amy was (a, no) _____ real
  surprise because she had been *cognizant* all along of what
  we were up to.

earmark (*v.*) set aside for a specific use or recipient; **designate**;
ˈi(ə)r-ˌmärk **allocate**

5. Supporters of the school's athletic program are (angered, pleased) _____ that funds have been *earmarked* for a new scoreboard.

excoriate (*v.*)   denounce severely; **flay**; **berate**; **lambaste**
ek-'skȯr-ē-ˌāt

6. The supervisor *excoriated* three workers on the night shift for (excellence, negligence) _____ in the performance of their duties.

fabricate (*v.*)   make up for the purpose of deception; **forge**; **fake**
'fab-ri-ˌkāt

7. The defendant was (acquitted, convicted) _____ mainly because it was shown that some of the evidence against her had been *fabricated*.

flabbergast (*v.*)   overwhelm with shock, surprise, or wonder;
'flab-ər-ˌgast   **dumbfound**; **amaze**; **astound**

8. The official was so *flabbergasted* by my request that he (dropped, put on) _____ his glasses.

implausible (*adj.*)   seemingly unreasonable or unworthy of be-
im-'plȯ-zə-bəl   lief; **improbable**; **incredible**

9. The story was so *implausible* that most people assumed it was (true, false) _____ .

inarticulate (*adj.*)   incapable of speech, especially under stress or
ˌin-är-'tik-yə-lət   emotion; **mute**; **speechless**

10. Awed by the grandeur of the scenery, we were almost *inarticulate*; (much, little) _____ was said.

SENTENCE COMPLETION 1–10: Enter the required lesson words.

1. When the company became _____ of an omission in the tax return it had just filed, it sent in a(n) _____**ed** return.

2. Inez was _____**ed** when asked if she would accept the directorship, and for a few moments she was _____ .

3. The commissioner was _____**d** by the press for using funds _____**ed** for road repairs to take trips to vacation resorts.

4. The suspect may have _____**d** the story about his escape from strangers who had kidnapped him for no apparent reason; it sounds so _____ .

5. There was a(n) _____ exchange between our coach and an umpire whom he accused of _____ against our team.

 SYNONYM ROUNDUP 1–10: Each line, when completed, should have three synonyms. Enter the missing letters.

---

1. f __ ke   f __ rge   f __ br __ cate

2. ch __ nge   rephr __ se   amen __

3. c __ gn __ zant   consc __ __ us   aw __ re

4. impr __ b __ ble   incred __ ble   impl __ __ sible

5. stin __ ing   c __ __ stic   acr __ m __ nious

6. fl __ y   exc __ riate   b __ rate

7. __ __ rmark   all __ cate   desi __ nate

8. __ ne-sidedness   p __ rt __ ality   b __ as

9. __ __ articulate   sp __ __ chless   m __ te

10. ast __ __ nd   fl __ bberg __ st   dum __ found

 LESSON WORDS 11–20: Pronounce the word, spell it, study its meanings, and finish the sentence that follows it.

---

onslaught (*n.*) especially fierce attack; **assault**; **offensive**
'än-ˌslȯt

   11. A long series of mild winters had (well, ill) _____ prepared the residents for the *onslaughts* of severe ones.

optimistic (*adj.*) inclined to make the most favorable interpreta-
ˌäp-tə-'mis-tik tion of actions or events, or to anticipate the best possible outcome; **hopeful**; **sanguine**; **upbeat**

   12. The sportswriter's *optimistic* comments about the prospects for our team made our spirits (soar, plummet) _____ .

panacea (*n.*) remedy for all ills or difficulties; **cure-all**; **elixir**
ˌpan-ə-'sē-ə

   13. The new remedy at first was (deplored, hailed) _____ as a *panacea* for irritations of the skin.

portend (*v.*) give an omen or anticipatory sign of; **bode**; **sig-**
pȯr-'tend **nify**; **foreshadow**; **presage**

   14. The sharp (increase, drop) _____ in the force of the wind in the last hour *portends* an end to the storm.

short-sighted (*adj.*)   unable to see far; lacking foresight; **near-**
'shòrt-'sīt-əd   **sighted**; **myopic**

> 15. It was *short-sighted* to take half of the money earmarked
>   for necessities and use it to buy (lottery tickets, food)
>
>   _____ .

stall (*v.*)   come to a standstill; **stop**; **halt**
'stòl

> 16. The occupants would have been in extreme danger if their
>
>   car had *stalled* (on, past) _____ the railroad
>   tracks.

supersede (*v.*)   force out of use as inferior; **displace**; **supplant**;
ˌsü-pər-'sēd   **replace**

> 17. The (stagecoach, airplane) _____ was
>   *superseded* by the automobile.

unparalleled (*adj.*)   having no *parallel* (equal or match); **unique**;
ˌən-'par-ə-ˌleld   **matchless**

> 18. Franklin D. Roosevelt's election to a fourth term as Presi-
>   dent was *unparalleled*—such a thing had (seldom, never)
>
>   _____ happened before.

untenable (*adj.*)   not capable of being defended; **unjustifiable**;
ˌən-'ten-ə-bəl   **indefensible**

> 19. If you arrive at the theater late and find someone in your
>
>   reserved seat, (that person's, your) _____
>   claim to the seat is *untenable*.

vindicate (*v.*)   free from any question of error, dishonor, guilt, or
'vin-də-ˌkāt   negligence; **exonerate**; **absolve**; **exculpate**

> 20. The executive whose management ability was under at-
>
>   tack (welcomed, opposed) _____ the
>   probe because he felt it would *vindicate* him.

E **SENTENCE COMPLETION 11–20:** Enter the required lesson words from D, above.

---

1. Fulton was assailed as a(n) _____ fool for proposing to build a steamboat, but subsequent events _____**d** his wisdom.

2. Recent developments have made us _____; we believe they _____ a peaceful and lasting solution to the bitter conflict.

3. The notion that money alone will solve all the world's problems is _____; money will help considerably, but is by no means a(n) _____.

4. Ever since the _____ policy of skimping on maintenance and repairs was _____**d**, there have been few equipment breakdowns.

5. In 1941, a major German _____ that swiftly overran much of European Russia _____**ed** outside Moscow in the middle of a severe winter.

  SYNONYM ROUNDUP 11–20: Enter the missing letters.

---

11. st __ p	h __ lt	st __ ll
12. h __ peful	opt __ m __ stic	sang __ __ ne
13. abs __ lve	ex __ n __ rate	vind __ cate
14. ass __ __ lt	off __ nsive	onsl __ __ ght
15. m __ tchless	__ __ paralleled	__ nique
16. indefens __ ble	__ __ tenable	unjustif __ able
17. s __ gnify	p __ rtend	b __ de
18. c __ re-all	pana __ ea	el __ x __ r
19. n __ __ rsighted	sh __ rt-sighted	m __ opic
20. super __ ede	d __ splace	s __ pplant

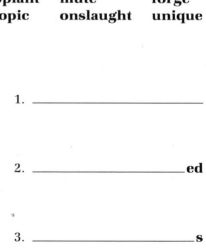

G   **SYNONYMS:** To avoid repetition, replace the boldfaced word with a synonym from the vocabulary list below.

---

stinging	incredible	supplant	mute	forge
sanguine	foreshadow	myopic	onslaught	unique

1. Andrew Carnegie's rise from rags to riches is not **unparalleled**; numerous parallels exist in America.

   1. _____

2. Many of the employees in the shop have said they would retire if their present supervisor is **superseded**.

   2. _____**ed**

3. The physician says the steady improvement in the patient's condition is a good portent; it **portends** a full recovery.

   3. _____**s**

4. In stressful situations, even the most articulate persons in the world may be momentarily **inarticulate**.

5. Those who persist in being **optimistic** when there are definitely no grounds whatsoever for optimism are clearly deluding themselves.

6. So extreme was the acrimony between the rivals that one more **acrimonious** remark from either of them might have led to violence.

7. Jim claimed the confession he allegedly signed had been **fabricated** by his enemies, and experts later confirmed it was indeed a fabrication.

8. The stronghold was assaulted simultaneously from all sides but was not taken, though thousands perished in the **assault**.

9. How can anyone put any faith in the **implausible** account that they have given? There is not one shred of plausibility in it.

10. Leaving school now to take a steady job may have some short-term advantage, but in the long run, it could be **short-sighted**.

4. _____

5. _____

6. _____

7. _____**d**

8. _____

9. _____

10. _____

ANTONYMS: In the blank space in each sentence below, enter the word most nearly the antonym of the boldfaced word or words. Choose your antonyms from the following list.

flabbergast	convict
invent	defensible
lambaste	harmonious
farsighted	impartiality
pessimistic	unaware

1. Only recently did she become **cognizant** of some important facts about exercise that she had been _____ of.

2. Try to avoid extremes; be neither **unduly inclined to anticipate the best**, nor _____.

3. In a true democracy, the courts show _____ to all and **bias** to none.

4. Instead of taking the **myopic** view, try to be _____ .

5. The civilian expecting to be **praised to the skies** for trying to put out the fire, was _____**d** for not summoning the fire department at once.

6. Their **acrimonious** negotiations being over, labor and management have resumed their former _____ relationship.

7. Someone else must have _____**ed** that tale—I did **not fabricate** it.

8. The coach was **not astounded** by the outcome, having predicted my success, but I was _____**ed**.

9. Their position being **untenable**, they retreated under cover of darkness to more _____ ground.

10. The suspect's attorney, maintaining her client's innocence, made a final appeal to the jury not to _____ him, but to **vindicate** him.

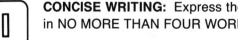

CONCISE WRITING: Express the thought of each sentence in NO MORE THAN FOUR WORDS.

1. The quarrel that they had with each other was full of harsh and biting sharpness.

   _____

2. I was not able to utter a single solitary word.

   _____

3. Those who serve in the capacity of referee must avoid being partial to one side or the other.

   _____

4. The excuses that they offered seemed to lack the ring of truth or credibility.

   _____

5. Under normal circumstances, we are inclined to make the most favorable interpretations of actions or events.

   _____

6. Those who lead others should have the ability to look ahead into the future to see what the impact of any action they are considering might be.

   _____

   _____

 ANALOGIES: Which lettered pair of words—**a, b, c, d,** or **e**— most nearly has the same relationship as the numbered pair? Enter the letter of your answer in the space provided.

1. BODE : PORTEND

   _a._ raze : build   _b._ taint : decontaminate
   _c._ mar : embellish   _d._ vie : contend
   _e._ foment : quell   1. _____

2. STALL : IMMOBILE

   _a._ expand : size   _b._ fade : dim
   _c._ accumulate : volume   _d._ abate : severity
   _e._ rankle : agreeable   2. _____

3. ONSLAUGHT : WITHSTAND

    a. envelope : seal   *b.* water : boil
    c. feud : resolve   *d.* dessert : consume
    e. button : press   3. _____

4. EARMARK : ALLOCATE

    a. expunge : obliterate   *b.* alienate : befriend
    c. upbraid : laud   *d.* arouse : allay
    e. validate : abrogate   4. _____

5. CAUSTIC : STING

    a. unambiguous : confuse   *b.* immortal : wither
    c. unobtrusive : interfere   *d.* innocuous : hurt
    e. mild : soothe   5. _____

6. MYOPIC : FORESIGHT

    a. mediocre : excellence   *b.* well-to-do : resources
    c. humane : compassion   *d.* impatient : error
    e. civil : courtesy   6. _____

7. COGNIZANT : AWARENESS

    a. brash : caution   *b.* irrepressible : restraint
    c. prudent : discretion   *d.* unprincipled : conscience
    e. unapprehensive : dread   7. _____

8. IMPARTIAL : BIAS

    a. lenient : forbearance   *b.* gregarious : company
    c. ardent : devotion   *d.* indifferent : apathy
    e. irreproachable : fault   8. _____

9. OPTIMIST : UPBEAT

    a. alarmist : reliable   *b.* prankster : innocuous
    c. nonconformist : compliant   *d.* trespasser : intrusive
    e. partisan : neutral   9. _____

10. UNPARALLELED : PEER

    a. rumored : significance   *b.* purposeful : objective
    c. inequitable : grievance   *d.* interminable : end
    e. condonable : excuse   10. _____

LESSON 12

 LESSON WORDS 1–10: Pronounce the word, spell it, study its meanings, and finish the sentence that follows it.

accolade (*n.*) anything done or given as a sign of great respect,
ˈak-ə-ˌlād approval, or appreciation; **honor**; **award**; **praise**;
kudos

 1. The skater earned many *accolades* for her (unparalleled, uninspiring) _____ performance.

allure (*n.*) power of attraction; **appeal**; **fascination**; **charm**
ə-ˈlu̇r

 2. The *allure* of the sea made us view the impending voyage with (joy, dread) _____ .

arch (*adj.*) most important; **main**; **chief**; **principal**
ˈärch

 3. Tickets will be (hard, easy) _____ to get for the upcoming game between the world champions and their *arch* foes.

brace (*v.*) make ready for an impact or shock; **steady**; **prepare**;
ˈbrās **steel**; **fortify**

 4. *Brace* yourselves; we're approaching a stretch of (level, rough) _____ road.

carnage (*n.*) great and bloody slaughter; **massacre**; **blood-**
ˈkär-nij **shed**; **butchery**

 5. Those who strongly (favored, opposed) _____ the continuation of the war repeatedly called attention to its *carnage*.

109

cherish (*v.*) hold dear; **appreciate**; **prize**; **treasure**; **esteem**
'cher-ish

> 6. We were (sad, glad) _____ to hear the people next door are moving; they are neighbors that we *cherish*.

decisive (*adj.*) showing firmness or determination; **resolute**;
di-'sī-siv   **determined**

> 7. The *decisive* manner in which the director gave the order was a sign that she would allow (some, no) _____ exceptions.

engross (*v.*) occupy completely; take the whole attention of; **absorb**; **engage**
in-'grōs

> 8. She was so *engrossed* by the book that she almost failed to (turn the page, answer the doorbell) _____ .

ephemeral (*adj.*) lasting a very short time; **transient**; **short-lived**
i-'fem-ə-rəl

> 9. If you were king or queen for a (decade, day) _____, your authority would be *ephemeral*.

erode (*v.*) wear away gradually by constant friction; **diminish**; **undermine**
i-'rōd

> 10. The new ruler's (swift, hesitant) _____ responses in crisis after crisis have *eroded* the people's confidence in his ability to govern.

SENTENCE COMPLETION 1–10: Enter the required lesson words.

---

1. Doug is now so _____**ed** in sports that he seldom even looks at his stamp collection, which once had an irresistible _____ for him.

2. Unless we take _____ action to keep intoxicated

   drivers off the roads, the _____ on the highways

   is certain to continue.

3. The _____ that the athletes _____**ed**

   most was the parade they were given down Fifth Avenue after

   they won the world championship.

4. Our optimism began to _____ when we realized

   that the recession we were in was not going to be a(n)

   _____ problem.

5. In 1588, the English _____**d** themselves for an ex-

   pected invasion by the Spaniards, their _____ rivals

   for control of the seas.

SYNONYM ROUNDUP 1–10: Each line, when completed, should have three synonyms. Enter the missing letters.

---

1. ch __ __ f   arc __   princip __ __

2. eng __ ge   abs __ rb   __ __ gross

3. tr __ __ sure   est __ __ m   ch __ r __ sh

4. prep __ re   st __ __ l   br __ ce

5. d __ termined   res __ lute   dec __ sive

6. bl __ __ dshed   c __ rnage   massac __ __

7. acc __ l __ de   k __ d __ s   h __ n __ r

8. d __ minish   __ __ dermine   er __ de

9. app __ __l   all __ re   fas __ ination

10. sh __ rt-l __ ved   trans __ __ nt   eph __ m __ ral

D

LESSON WORDS 11–20: Pronounce the word, spell it, study its meanings, and finish the sentence that follows it.

---

nimble (*adj.*) quick and light in movement; **agile**; **active**
'nim-bəl

> 11. Being *nimble*, Nick had no trouble (leaping the puddle, finishing the asparagus) _____ .

pacific (*adj.*) not warlike; **nonviolent**; **peaceable**
pə-'sif-ik

> 12. The (impenetrable, unfenced) _____ property line separating the neighbors is a sign of their *pacific* relations with one another.

pry (*v.*) inquire impertinently into private matters; **snoop**; **peep**
'prī

> 13. To protect yourself from *prying* fellow passengers, you should not read your (confidential, junk) _____ mail on a bus or train.

squirm (*v.*) twist about like a worm; **wriggle**; **writhe**; **fidget**
'skwərm

> 14. If you were in a(n) (uneasy, comfortable) _____ position, you wouldn't have been *squirming*.

tenacious (*adj.*) characterized by a firm hold; **strong**; **sturdy**;
tə-'nā-shəs   **secure**

> 15. Their grip on first place is so *tenacious* that it would be (a, no) _____ snap for any rival to break it.

umbrage (*n.*) feeling of annoyance at some real or fancied slight
'əm-brij   or insult; **offense**; **resentment**; **displeasure**

16. Who wouldn't have taken *umbrage* at the (warm, cool)

_____ welcome we were accorded?

uncanny (*adj.*) beyond what is normal or expected; so remark-
ˌən-'kan-ē   able as to seem to have a supernatural origin;
                weird; **eerie**; **mysterious**

17. The hound's *uncanny* ability to follow a trail is its cardinal

(asset, liability) _____ .

undercover (*adj.*) acting or done in secret; **surreptitious**;
ˌən-dər-'kəv-ər   **clandestine**

18. When Holmes was about to leave on an *undercover* inves-

tigation, he (doffed, donned) _____ a disguise.

usurp (*v.*) seize and hold or use (an office, place, or power) with-
yü-'sərp   out right; **arrogate**; **appropriate**; **assume**

19. If a child needs punishment, a parent should administer it;

a (mother, stranger) _____ should not
usurp that responsibility.

vanquish (*v.*) subdue completely in battle or in a contest; **con-
'vaŋ-kwish   quer**; **crush**; **defeat**

20. The victors were assailed for (respecting, looting)

_____ the art treasures of the nations
they had *vanquished*.

E **SENTENCE COMPLETION 11–20:** Enter the required lesson words from D, above.

---

1. From a(n) _____ informant, the monarch

learned that one of his ministers was plotting to _____

the throne.

2. The two young antagonists _____**ed** in the _____ grip of the brawny adults who had separated them.

3. Atalanta was renowned for her _____ ability to elude all who pursued her; no other Greek maiden was so _____ as she.

4. We take _____ at the shameless attempts of busybodies to _____ into our personal affairs.

5. Determined to _____ their opponents, they are turning a deaf ear to those who urge a(n) _____ resolution to the bitter conflict.

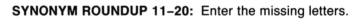

F   SYNONYM ROUNDUP 11–20: Enter the missing letters.

---

11. sn __ __ p   p __ __ p   __ ry

12. def __ __ t   cr __ sh   v __ nquish

13. act __ ve   nimb __ __   ag __ le

14. wr __ ggle   __ rithe   sq __ __ rm

15. peac __ __ ble   pac __ f __ c   nonv __ __ lent

16. st __ rdy   s __ cure   tenac __ __ __ s

17. us __ rp   arr __ gate   approp __ __ __ te

18. w __ __ rd   __ __ canny   __ __ rie

19. off __ nse   __ mbr __ ge   __ __ __ pleasure

20. __ __ dercover   cl __ nd __ stine   s __ __ reptitious

SYNONYMS: To avoid repetition, replace the boldfaced word with a synonym from the vocabulary list below.

---

kudos	appropriate	arch	secure	clandestine
agile	fortify	fascination	snoop	unvanquished

1. Every one of our rivals suffered at least one defeat during the season; we, alone, were **undefeated**.

1. _____

2. Probers uncovered much valuable information as a result of their **undercover** investigation.

2. _____

3. If he hadn't stumbled, our nimble pass-receiver could easily have eluded his less **nimble** pursuer.

3. _____

4. Macbeth was a murderer and a usurper; he slew the king and **usurped** the throne, which rightfully belonged to the king's son.

4. _____d

5. The company has taken steps to protect its secrets from prying eyes; it is concerned that industrial spies may be **prying** into its files.

5. _____ing

6. Bowing to acknowledge the accolade of the audience, the conductor motioned the musicians to rise to share in the **accolade**.

6. _____

7. Many losers are too weak to resist the **allure** of gambling; the hope of big winnings eventually lures them back.

7. _____

8. The tenacity of the insurgents is undiminished; in fact, their hold on the peninsula is even more **tenacious** than before.

8. _____

9. The Hawks are the team we are principally concerned about; they are our **principal** opponents.

9. _____

10. **Brace** yourself with a bowl of bracing hot soup before going out to resume your snow-removal chores.

10. _____

 ANTONYMS: In the blank space in each sentence below, enter the word most nearly the antonym of the boldfaced word. Choose your antonyms from the following list.

| distract | inactive | perpetual | open | restore |
| warlike | dishonor | lax | scorn | allure |

1. Residents are jubilant that parts of the beach **eroded** by recent coastal storms have been _____**d**.

2. It is unwise for supervisors to maintain either very _____ or very **tenacious** control over everything going on in the shop.

3. The citizens want a(n) _____ investigation, not an **undercover** one.

4. Entomology, the study of insects, has **no attraction** for me, but for my cousin it has an irresistible

_____.

5. The program **engrossed** my attention until the din from the outside _____ **ed** it.

6. We are delighted that the recent annoyance was only **ephemeral**; we had feared it might become a(n) _____ nuisance.

7. The tennis star has been _____ since undergoing surgery, but it is expected she soon will be on the courts, as **nimble** as ever.

8. The new rulers are _____ **ing** values that their predecessors had **cherished**.

9. How odd that a nation should have turned _____ so soon after declaring its **pacific** intentions!

10. It is sad that someone who has won many an **accolade** should have brought _____ on himself.

CONCISE WRITING: Express the thought of each sentence in NO MORE THAN FOUR WORDS.

---

1. Beaches are being gradually worn away by the constant friction of the wind and the sea.

---

2. What is it that is causing you to twist about like a worm?

---

3. People who are busybodies keep on inquiring impertinently into matters that are no concern of theirs.

---

4. The foresight that she has shown is beyond what is normal or expected.

---

5. Those who are hotheaded are quick to show annoyance at some real or fancied slight or insult.

_____

6. The stories that they told us commanded our entire attention.

_____

 ANALOGIES: Which lettered pair of words—**a, b, c, d,** or **e**— most nearly has the same relationship as the numbered pair? Enter the letter of your answer in the space provided.

1. NOBEL PRIZE : ACCOLADE

    a. conviction : reputation   *b.* spring : season
    c. roadblock : delay   *d.* beverage : milk
    e. blunder : embarrassment   1. _____

2. ARCH : FOREMOST

    a. myopic : farsighted   *b.* trite : stale
    c. eloquent : inarticulate   *d.* ignorant : cognizant
    e. pessimistic : sanguine   2. _____

3. PACIFIST : CARNAGE

    a. scholar : knowledge   *b.* despot : domination
    c. manufacturer : productivity   *d.* teacher : ignorance
    e. advertiser : sales   3. _____

4. ITCH : SQUIRM

    a. reminder : forget   *b.* nightmare : sleep
    c. emergency : procrastinate   *d.* blizzard : travel
    e. taunt : bristle   4. _____

5. KEEPSAKE : CHERISH

    a. rudeness : tolerate   *b.* ordeal : relish
    c. windfall : expect   *d.* compliment : resent
    e. folly : rue   5. _____

6. HARE : NIMBLENESS

    a. hawk : peace

    c. bulldog : tenacity

    e. garter snake : venomousness

    b. dove : belligerence

    d. daredevil : timidity

    6. _____

7. INDECISIVE : FIRMNESS

    a. partial : bias

    c. vain : conceit

    e. scrupulous : integrity

    b. apathetic : concern

    d. gregarious : sociability

    7. _____

8. ALLURING : RESIST

    a. enigmatic : diagnose

    c. condonable : forgive

    e. delectable : digest

    b. explicit : interpret

    d. unforgettable : recall

    8. _____

9. EPHEMERAL : LAST

    a. dramatic : startle

    c. vexatious : nettle

    e. capricious : change

    b. shocking : appall

    d. implausible : convince

    9. _____

10. LAUD : KUDOS

    a. implicate : innocence

    c. thwart : frustration

    e. excoriate : commendation

    b. interrogate : information

    d. alienate : friendship

    10. _____

LESSON 13

LESSON WORDS 1–10: Pronounce the word, spell it, study its meanings, and finish the sentence that follows it.

amnesty (*n.*) act granting forgiveness for past offenses to a large
ˈam-nə-stē   group of individuals; **pardon**; **absolution**

1. In its current *amnesty*, the library is (doubling, forgiving)

_____ the fines on overdue books.

burgeon (*v.*) grow or develop rapidly; **flourish**; **expand**
ˈbər-jən

2. The town is *burgeoning* because of the (abundance, pauc-

ity) _____ of jobs in the area.

capitulate (*v.*) cease resisting; **yield**; **acquiesce**; **surrender**
kə-ˈpich-ə-ˌlāt

3. The resisters did not *capitulate* because their grievances

had been (redressed, ignored) _____ .

contemplate (*v.*) look at or view with continued attention; **con-**
ˈkänt-əm-ˌplāt   **sider**; **ponder**; **study**

4. We *contemplated* the rainbow for an uninterrupted fif-

teen (minutes, seconds) _____ .

daunt (*v.*) lessen the courage of; **cow**; **intimidate**; **dishearten**;
ˈdȯnt   **dismay**

5. Refusing to be *daunted*, the small dog (backed away, stood

its ground) _____ .

120

deadpan (*adj.*)   marked by a careful pretense of seriousness or
'ded-ˌpan   calm detachment; showing no emotional or personal involvement; **expressionless**; **vacant**;
blank

6. The defendant's *deadpan* expression offered (no, a)

_____ clue as to how he felt about the verdict.

drench (*v.*)   wet thoroughly; **soak**; **saturate**; **deluge**
'drench

7. If not for her (diet, umbrella) _____, she
would have been *drenched*.

forebear (*n.*)   (usually used in the plural) ancestor generally more
'fȯr-ˌbe(ə)r   remote than a grandparent; **antecedent**; **fore-
father**

8. When we mention our *forebears*, we are referring to the

distant (future, past) _____ .

harvest (*n.*)   act, process, or occasion of gathering a crop; **reap-
'här-vəst   ing**; **ingathering**

9. Demand for farm workers (plummets, soars) _____
after each *harvest*.

incentive (*n.*)   something that incites to determination or action;
in-'sent-iv   **motive**; **stimulus**; **encouragement**

10. (Lower, Higher) _____ interest rates are an *incentive* for the bank's savers to deposit more money.

SENTENCE COMPLETION 1–10: Enter the required lesson
words.

---

1. The upcoming _____ is likely to be smaller than

usual because of the heavy rains that _____**ed** the

crops soon after planting time.

2. The forthcoming tax cut will be a(n) _____

   for consumers to buy more of the things they need, and as a

   result, business is expected to _____ .

3. Many of us would surely have been _____**ed** by the

   awesome obstacles that confronted our _____**s**

   in their daily lives.

4. Though they have been offered _____ , the rebels

   thus far have refused to _____ .

5. As I _____**d** the cards I was holding, I

   stole glances at my arch opponent's _____ face,

   from which I learned absolutely nothing.

 SYNONYM ROUNDUP 1–10: Each line, when completed, should have three synonyms. Enter the missing letters.

---

1. cons __ der   p __ nder   cont __ mpl __ te

2. __ oak   sat __ rate   dr __ nch

3. h __ rvest   __ eaping   __ __ gathering

4. m __ tive   stim __ lus   __ __ centive

5. bl __ nk   expression __ __ __ __ __   d __ __ __ dpan

6. p __ rd __ n   __ mnesty   __ __ solution

7. anc __ st __ r   foreb __ __ r   ant __ c __ dent

8. d __ __ nt   __ __ __ hearten   int __ m __ date

9. s __ rr __ nder   c __ p __ t __ late __ __ quiesce

10. exp __ nd   fl __ __ rish   burg __ __ n

LESSON WORDS 11–20: Pronounce the word, spell it, study its meanings, and finish the sentence that follows it.

---

intrigue (*v.*) **fascinate**; **excite**; arouse the interest or curiosity
in-'trēg   of

11. Who would not be *intrigued* by a (commonplace, myste-
rious) _____ happening?

noisome (*adj.*) offensive to the senses, especially the sense of
'nŏi-səm   smell; **malodorous**; **disgusting**

12. The more *noisome* the air quality of a neighborhood, the
more (attractive, uninviting) _____ it
is to live in.

ostentatious (*adj.*) fond of or marked by *ostentation* (vain and
͵äs-tən-'tā-shəs   unnecessary show for the purpose of attracting attention); **showy**; **pretentious**

13. *Ostentatious* dressers want to be (ignored, noticed)
_____ .

pilfer (*v.*) obtain by petty theft in small quantities; **steal**; **pur-**
'pil-fər   **loin**; **appropriate**

14. The new homes may cost (less, more) _____ because building materials are being *pilfered* from the construction sites.

revel (*v.*) take part in a *revel* (a usually wild celebration); **ca-**
'rev-əl   **rouse**; **frolic**

15. Many fans *reveled* the night away after their team's spec-
tacular (defeat, victory) _____ .

undermine (*v.*) weaken or cause to collapse by removing under-
ən-dər-'mīn   lying support; **cripple**; **disable**

16. The senator's reelection campaign was *undermined* when
he (received, lost) _____ the support of two
powerful community organizations.

unseemly (*adj.*) not in keeping with established standards of
ən-'sēm-lē   good form and taste; **unbecoming**; **inappropriate**; **indecorous**

17. It would have been *unseemly* for us to (wait our turn, push ahead of others) _____ .

uproarious (*adj.*) causing or accompanied by an uproar; **noisy**;
ˌə-'prȯr-ē-əs   **tumultuous**; **rackety**

18. It was truly an *uproarious* meeting; (pandemonium, tranquility) _____ reigned.

voluble (*adj.*) characterized by a continuous and ready flow of
'väl-yə-bəl   words; **fluent**; **talkative**; **loquacious**

19. Our *voluble* host was (never, often) _____ at a loss for words.

voluminous (*adj.*) sufficient to fill many volumes; **copious**;
və-'lü-mə-nəs   **lengthy**

20. The trial may take a couple of (days, months) _____ because the evidence is *voluminous*.

 SENTENCE COMPLETION 11–20: Enter the required lesson words from D, above.

---

1. It is _____ to _____ after an easy victory over a weak rival plagued by a succession of unfortunate injuries.

2. _____**d** by World War II, she spends a good deal of time at her local library, which has a(n) _____ amount of information on the subject.

3. Residents are _____ in their demand for

   a cleanup of the abandoned industrial site from which

   _____ odors are emanating.

4. The comedians' efforts to _____ a piece of steak from

   the lion's cage at feeding time in the zoo provoked the movie-

   goers to _____ laughter.

5. She felt that to wear her medals would be _____

   and might _____ the close relationship she

   had with her valued friends.

 SYNONYM ROUNDUP 11–20: Enter the missing letters.

---

11. weak __ n   dis __ ble   __ __ __ __ __ mine

12. fas __ inate   exc __ te   intrig __ __

13. n __ __ sy   __ __ roarious   t __ m __ lt __ ous

14. talk __ tive   v __ l __ ble   fl __ ent

15. show __   __ st __ ntatious   pr __ t __ ntious

16. st __ __ l   p __ lf __ r   p __ rloin

17. fr __ lic   r __ v __ l   car __ __ se

18. disg __ sting   n __ __ some   __ __ __ odorous

19. l __ ngthy   c __ pious   v __ l __ minous

20. uns __ __ mly   __ __ becoming   ind __ c __ rous

SYNONYMS: To avoid repetition, replace the boldfaced word with a synonym from the vocabulary list below.

malodorous	consider	carouse	reaping	loquacious
yield		fascinate	purloin	soak	dismay

1. We have several **voluble** members; in fact, two are so voluble that, if unrestrained, they would give no one else a chance to speak.

2. **Daunted** by the approaching storm, some fled to inland sanctuaries, but the undaunted majority rode out the crisis in their homes.

3. Harvest time is the season of the **harvest** of crops.

4. The shoplifter caught with the **pilfered** merchandise was found to have had several earlier arrests for pilfering.

5. **Contemplate** what you are about to do; do not rush into anything without adequate contemplation of the likely consequences.

6. Our clothes were **drenched** when we raced for shelter from the drenching rain.

7. The few surviving defenders refused to **capitulate**, though advised by their government that their capitulation would be no shame.

8. The winners at the polls **reveled** past midnight; for some of them, it was almost dawn before the revelry ended.

1. _____

2. _____ **ed**

3. _____

4. _____ **ed**

5. _____

6. _____ **ed**

7. _____

8. _____ **d**

9. I did not find that movie in-
triguing, but several of my
friends were **intrigued** by
it.

9. _____d

10. The residents of the bay area
are frequently annoyed by
the **noisome** air coming
from the direction of the pol-
luted water.

10. _____

ANTONYMS: In the blank space in each sentence below,
enter the word most nearly the antonym of the boldfaced
word. Choose your antonyms from the following list.

**bore   meager inarticulate withstand unpretentious
enhearten proper disincentive fragrant   reinforce**

1. In this **noisome** place, about a hundred years ago, birds sang,

   and the air was _____ with the aroma
   of flowering shrubs.

2. This loud tie would be too **ostentatious** for a(n)

   _____ person like your brother Roy.

3. While almost all of us are working to _____
   our community's reputation for politeness, a few, by tactless
   behavior, can seriously **undermine** it.

4. The police have a(n) _____ file on one
   of the suspects but a **voluminous** one on the other.

5. It is **unseemly** for husband and wife to quarrel noisily in
   public; if they have a disagreement, their home is the

   _____ place to deal with it.

6. Some spectators **capitulated** to the wind and took shelter, but

   others were able to _____ its fury till
   the game was over.

7. **Daunted** by their failure to sight land, the crew was about
   to turn home when the sudden appearance of birds

   _____**ed** them.

8. Why is it that on some topics you are remarkably **voluble**, but on others you are almost _____?

9. The answer is quite simple: some topics **intrigue** me; others _____ me.

10. Just as lower prices are an **encouragement** for shoppers to buy, so higher prices may be a(n) _____.

 CONCISE WRITING: Express the thought of each sentence in NO MORE THAN FOUR WORDS.

---

1. Note that manner of hers that reveals no emotional or personal involvement whatsoever on her part.

_____

2. The community that we live in is developing at a rapid rate.

_____

3. Termites caused that house to collapse by eating their way through its supporting timbers.

_____

4. Many individuals were granted forgiveness for offenses that they had committed in the past.

_____

5. What are the subjects that arouse your interest or curiosity?

_____

6. There are people who are fond of vain and unnecessary show as a means of attracting attention to themselves.

_____

J

ANALOGIES: Which lettered pair of words—**a, b, c, d,** or **e**—most nearly has the same relationship as the numbered pair? Enter the letter of your answer in the space provided.

1. DRENCH : WET

   a. skim : read
   c. heat : cook
   e. taste : eat

   b. vanquish : subdue
   d. defrost : freeze

   1. _____

2. DAUNT : COURAGE

   a. laud : pride
   c. elevate : status
   e. disparage : reputation

   b. intimidate : anxiety
   d. vindicate : esteem

   2. _____

3. REVELER : MERRYMAKING

   a. pacifist : war
   c. conspirator : intrigue
   e. nonparticipant : competition

   b. rebel : establishment
   d. conservative : innovation

   3. _____

4. UNAMBITIOUS : INCENTIVE

   a. reprehensible : blame
   c. distraught : concern
   e. indulgent : leeway

   b. capricious : fickleness
   d. myopic : foresight

   4. _____

5. HARVEST : CROP

   a. survey : information
   c. planting : soil
   e. confession : wrongdoing

   b. meal : nourishment
   d. breach : law

   5. _____

6. COMMOTION : UPROARIOUS

   a. affliction : painless
   c. boon : lamentable
   e. abnormality : typical

   b. quip : humorless
   d. fiasco : ridiculous

   6. _____

7. FOREBEAR : DESCENDANT

   a. vendor : retailer
   c. novice : tyro
   e. scoffer : flouter

   b. antagonist : supporter
   d. enthusiast : zealot

   7. _____

8. PILFER : STEAL

    a. loathe : dislike   *b.* scrutinize : examine
    c. nibble : eat   *d.* admire : like
    e. seize : take   8. _____

9. OSTENTATION : FOIBLE

    a. shoe : moccasin   *b.* island : peninsula
    c. barge : transportation   *d.* ambiguity : misunderstanding
    e. termite : insect   9. _____

10. NOISOME : SMELL

    a. melodious : hearing   *b.* attractive : sight
    c. thorny : touch   *d.* palatable : taste
    e. equitable : fairness   10. _____

LESSON 14

 LESSON WORDS 1–10: Pronounce the word, spell it, study its meanings, and finish the sentence that follows it.

abstemious (*adj.*) sparing or moderate in consuming food or al-
ab-'stē-mē-əs   cohol; **sober**; **temperate**; **self-restraining**

1. The (smaller, larger) _____ than usual por-
   tions were easy for the patient to adjust to, since she had
   always been *abstemious.*

anomaly (*n.*) deviation from the common rule; **abnormality**;
ə-'näm-ə-lē   **irregularity**

2. A (palm tree, snowstorm) _____ would
   be an *anomaly* in the tropics.

assuage (*v.*) make milder or less severe; **ease**; **relieve**
ə-'swāj

3. The animal's hunger seems to be *assuaged*; it is (still, done)
   _____ eating.

disaffect (*v.*) make discontented or disloyal; **estrange**; **alienate**
dis-ə-'fekt

4. The government's inexcusable (responsiveness, indifference) _____ to their needs
   has *disaffected* the residents of this community.

divest (*v.*) get rid of; **disencumber**; **free**; **rid**
dī-'vest

5. The retailing giant is *divesting* itself of those stores
   that have been consistently (profitable, unprofitable)
   _____ .

equilibrium (*n.*) **balance**; **stability**; **poise**; ability of the body
ˌē-kwə-ˈlib-rē-əm   to keep itself properly positioned

> 6. Sensing that he was about to (leave, fall)
>
> _____, he moved quickly to regain his *equilibrium*.

founder (*v.*) come to grief; **sink**; **fail**; **collapse**
ˈfaùn-dər

> 7. It would not be unusual for a ship in (shark-infested, un-
>
> charted) _____ waters to *founder*.

gorge (*v.*) eat greedily; fill with food; **glut**; **stuff**; **cram**
ˈgòrj

> 8. The food was so (unpalatable, tempting) _____
> that some of the guests could not help *gorging* themselves.

hefty (*adj.*) big and powerful; **husky**; **burly**
ˈhef-tē

> 9. Professional (football players, jockeys) _____
> tend to be *hefty*.

inebriated (*adj.*) exhilarated or confused by, or as if by, alcohol;
in-ˈē-brē-ˌāt-əd   **intoxicated**; **drunk**

> 10. *Inebriated* people are (more, less) _____ alert than
> usual.

  SENTENCE COMPLETION 1–10: Enter the required lesson
words.

---

1. My _____ assailant, who was about twice my weight,

   aimed a mighty blow that missed me so badly that he lost his

   _____ .

2. What can we do to _____ the hurt feelings of our

   _____ **ed** allies?

3. Many investors are ＿＿＿＿＿＿**ing** themselves of their

shares in the company for fear it may soon ＿＿＿＿＿＿.

4. Some say that humans are a(n) ＿＿＿＿＿＿ among

Earth's creatures in that they are about the only eaters that

＿＿＿＿＿＿ themselves.

5. The neighbors were shocked one day to find Mother Magloire,

whose ＿＿＿＿＿＿ nature was well known to

them, lying ＿＿＿＿＿＿ in the snow.

 SYNONYM ROUNDUP 1–10: Each line, when completed, should have three synonyms. Enter the missing letters.

---

1. b ＿ l ＿ nce   p ＿ ＿ se   equilibr ＿ ＿ m

2. s ＿ ber   abst ＿ m ＿ ous   t ＿ mp ＿ rate

3. b ＿ rly   ＿ usky   h ＿ fty

4. al ＿ ＿ nate   ＿ strange   dis ＿ ffect

5. s ＿ nk   f ＿ ＿ nder   f ＿ ＿ l

6. r ＿ d   d ＿ vest   ＿ ＿ ＿ encumber

7. e ＿ se   rel ＿ ＿ ve   ass ＿ ＿ ge

8. dr ＿ nk   ＿ ＿ toxicated   inebr ＿ ＿ ted

9. cr ＿ m   st ＿ ff   g ＿ rge

10. an ＿ m ＿ ly   ＿ ＿ regularity   ＿ ＿ normality

LESSON WORDS 11–20: Pronounce the word, spell it, study its meanings, and finish the sentence that follows it.

---

munificent (*adj.*)   characterized by or displaying great generos-
myù-'nif-ə-sənt   ity; **bountiful**; **generous**; **lavish**

   11. A *munificent* reward of ($5, $500) _____ is being offered for the return of the lost dog to its grieving owner.

paltry (*adj.*)   practically   worthless;   **insignificant**;   **meager**;
'pòl-trē   **measly**

   12. The employees have (no, a) _____ real grievance; they have been offered a *paltry* increase in wages.

pamper (*v.*)   treat with extreme or excessive care or attention; **in-**
'pam-pər   **dulge**; **coddle**; **spoil**

   13. Parents   who   *pamper*   their   children   (deny,   give)
_____ them whatever they ask for.

perturbation (*n.*)   state   of   being   *perturbed*   (agitated   or   dis-
ˌpərt-ər-'bā-shən   turbed); **agitation**; **disturbance**

   14. As we sailed (away from, toward) _____ the waterfall, the river's *perturbation* gradually subsided.

precursor (*n.*) person   or   thing   that   precedes;   **forerunner**;
prē-'kər-sər   **predecessor**

   15. (Dawn, Sunrise) _____ is a *precursor* of a new day.

prescient (*adj.*)   having *prescience* (knowledge of things before
'presh(-ē)-ənt   they happen or exist); **farseeing**; **foresighted**

   16. Of course, since we are not *prescient*, we had (an, no)
_____ idea you would be here tonight.

retrospect (*n.*) looking back on past events; **review**; **survey**;
ˈre-trə-ˌspekt   **reexamination**

> 17. The Declaration of Independence contains a *retrospect* of
> the (future, past) _____ relations between
> George III and the Thirteen Colonies.

trivia (*n. pl.*) little-known, trivial facts or details; unimportant
ˈtriv-ē-ə   matters; **trifles**; **trivialities**

> 18. Preoccupation with *trivia* is usually time (ill, well)
> _____ spent.

unleash (*v.*) let loose from, or as if from, a leash; **release**; **free**
ən-ˈlēsh

> 19. Aeolus, in Greek mythology, was the keeper of the unruly
> winds; when he *unleashed* them, the seas were (calm, per-
> ilous) _____ .

volatile (*adj.*) likely to shift quickly and unpredictably; **unsta-**
ˈväl-ət-ᵊl   **ble; explosive**
  or ˈväl-ə-ˌtīl

> 20. Because of the *volatile* international situation, there is a
> (relaxed, tense) _____ mood in world capi-
> tals tonight.

 SENTENCE COMPLETION 11–20: Enter the required lesson words from D, above.

---

1. In _____, I now see that I made a mistake

in not forewarning you about Henry's _____

temper.

2. The quadricycle, a _____ of the automobile,

did not _____ drivers; it offered them just a bicycle

seat.

3. Some who had made _____ gifts to the community fund expressed regret that this year they could offer only a _____ donation, or no gift at all.

4. Since the villagers around Mt. Vesuvius were not _____, they had no way of telling when that volcano would again _____ its fury on them.

5. To the _____ of many, so much of the meeting was taken up with _____ that there was little time to discuss truly serious problems.

 SYNONYM ROUNDUP 11–20: Enter the missing letters.

---

11. m __ __ ger   m __ __ sly   p __ ltry

12. rel __ __ se   fr __ __   __ __ leash

13. rev __ __ w   r __ tr __ spect   __ __ examination

14. p __ mper   c __ ddle   ind __ lge

15. tr __ via   tr __ fles   triv __ __ lities

16. ag __ tation   dist __ rbance   pert __ rbation

17. __ __ __ __ __ runner   pr __ de __ essor   prec __ rs __ r

18. m __ n __ ficent   b __ __ ntiful   g __ n __ rous

19. expl __ sive   __ __ stable   v __ l __ tile

20. __ __ __ __ __ sighted   presc __ __ nt   fars __ __ ing

G SYNONYMS: To avoid repetition, replace the boldfaced word with a synonym from the vocabulary list below.

generous	release	burly	alienate	intoxicated
stuff	collapse	agitation	spoil	foresighted

1. The blame for the poor records of pampered children belongs squarely on the shoulders of those who have been **pampering** them.

1. _____**ing**

2. Since inebriation is a major cause of highway carnage, **inebriated** drivers must be kept off the roads.

2. _____

3. Andrew Carnegie is remembered for his munificence; so many public libraries in American cities were started by his **munificent** bequests.

3. _____

4. We are perturbed by the news, and our **perturbation** is even greater when we realize we can do nothing about it.

4. _____

5. The **hefty** wrestler stunned his opponent with a hefty blow.

5. _____

6. Someone must have **unleashed** that dog from its leash.

6. _____**d**

7. The retired founder was saddened to learn that the company he had founded is about to **founder**.

7. _____

8. Our prescience about some matters is increasing; never before, for example, have we been so **prescient** about the weather.

8. _____

9. The fact that a few were gorging themselves with sweets, was no excuse for you, too, to **gorge** yourself.

9. _____

10. The company is less shocked by the disaffection of some of its loyal customers, than by its ignorance of what has **disaffected** them.

10. _____**d**

 ANTONYMS: In the blank space in each sentence below, enter the word most nearly the antonym of the boldfaced word. Choose your antonyms from the following list.

sober	**exacerbate**	**normal**	**ungiving**	**conciliate**
essential	**unprescient**	**stable**	**neglect**	**gluttonous**

1. If the senator had not _____**d** many of the **disaffected** voters, he would not have been reelected.

2. While the **abstemious** diners were partaking lightly of the delicious food, the _____ ones were gorging themselves with it.

3. The prices of fruits and vegetables, so **volatile** last month, are now comparatively _____ .

4. The proper way for dog lovers to care for their pets is neither to **pamper** nor to _____ them.

5. Ordinary humans, being _____ , have always stood in awe of their **farseeing** gods and goddesses.

6. Because of the famine, the stricken nation hopes its affluent neighbors will be **munificent** in their assistance, rather than

   _____ .

7. Briareus, the **anomalous** hundred-handed monster of ancient legend, would be much less interesting if he had only the

   _____ number of hands.

8. Sometimes, measures that we take to **assuage** our discomfort

   serve only to _____ it.

9. All the guests left the party _____ , except two who were detained by the host because they seemed **inebriated**.

10. Some of the details that others had considered **trivial** were, in

    our opinion, _____ .

 CONCISE WRITING: Express the thought of each sentence in NO MORE THAN FOUR WORDS.

---

1. Little-known, trivial facts or details can arouse people's interest or curiosity.

   _____

2. Dizziness affects our ability to keep the body properly positioned.

   _____

3. In its hiring practices, industry has a preference for applicants who are sparing in their consumption of alcohol.

   _____

4. Is it true that those who tell fortunes for a fee have knowledge of things before they happen or exist?

   _____

5. The opinion of the public is likely to shift quickly and unpredict-ably.

_____

6. The venture that you and I have been involved in is coming to grief.

_____

ANALOGIES: Which lettered pair of words—**a, b, c, d,** or **e**—most nearly has the same relationship as the numbered pair? Enter the letter of your answer in the space provided.

1. LIBERATOR : UNLEASH

   a. defector : remain   *b.* maverick : conform
   c. truant : attend   *d.* comedian : quip
   e. mentor : mislead   1. _____

2. HEFTY : STRENGTH

   a. nimble : agility   *b.* inarticulate : volubility
   c. sanguine : pessimism   *d.* acrimonious : friendliness
   e. relaxed : tension   2. _____

3. ANOMALOUS : NORMAL

   a. unambiguous : explicit   *b.* ephemeral : transient
   c. implausible : credible   *d.* unparalleled : matchless
   e. untenable : indefensible   3. _____

4. STUMBLE : EQUILIBRIUM

   a delude : trickery   *b.* nettle : irritation
   c. alienate : disaffection   *d.* burgeon : size
   e. despair : hope   4. _____

5. INEBRIETY : ALCOHOL

   a. insomnia : sleep   *b.* frugality : waste
   c. insensitivity : feeling   *d.* audacity : caution
   e. fatigue : exertion   5. _____

6. VOLATILE : EXPLODE

    a. intelligible : comprehend   *b.* tentative : change
    c. innocuous : offend   *d.* distinct : perplex
    e. engrossing : bore   6. _____

7. PHILANTHROPIST : MUNIFICENCE

    a. mediator : partiality   *b.* liar : mendacity
    c. craven : bravery   *d.* diplomat : indiscretion
    e. copycat : originality   7. _____

8. PITFALL : FOUNDER

    a. accolade : beam   *b.* compliment : bristle
    c. affliction : rejoice   *d.* blunder : embarrass
    e. slight : overlook   8. _____

9. DIVEST : DISENCUMBER

    a. cherish : relinquish   *b.* contemplate : skim
    c. evacuate : remain   *d.* peeve : irritate
    e. laud : lambaste   9. _____

10. INDULGENT : PAMPER

    a. perverse : listen   *b.* deadpan : smile
    c. selfless : exploit   *d.* staunch : defect
    e. garrulous : tire   10. _____

LESSON 15: REVIEW AND ENRICHMENT

CLOSE READING: Read the following statements. Then answer questions 1–10.

STATEMENTS

An eating contest in Damon Runyon's *A Piece of Pie* ended when Joel Duffle told the judges, "Gentlemen, I am licked. I cannot eat another mouthful."

Ralph Bunche won the 1950 Nobel Peace Prize for his successful mediation of the 1948–49 Arab-Israeli War.

Susan B. Anthony, who was arrested in 1872 for attempting to vote, devoted her life to gaining equal political rights for women.

In 1950, George Bernard Shaw (1856–1950) slipped, fell, and fractured his left thighbone while attempting to cut back a protruding branch in his garden.

Arriving hungry in Philadelphia, 17-year-old Benjamin Franklin (1706–90) bought and ate some bread, which then cost just a penny for a large loaf.

Cassandra's predictions always came true, yet none of her fellow Trojans ever believed her when she made them.

In Jonathan Swift's *Gulliver's Travels*, the six-inch Lilliputians were shocked when they saw Gulliver, an English sailor, asleep on their shore.

A revolt against Queen Liliuokalani of Hawaii in 1893 led to her dethronement.

In Victor Hugo's *Les Miserables*, an invention by ex-convict Jean Valjean brought good jobs and prosperity to an impoverished city.

As ruler of Scotland, Macbeth was so cruel and tyrannical that he turned the whole nation against him.

QUESTIONS

1. Who made an area burgeon?_____

2. Who purchased an essential commodity for a paltry sum? ____

3. Who was gorged? _____

4. Who was divested of authority? _____

5. Who disaffected an entire populace? _____

6. Who had a momentary loss of equilibrium? _____

7. Who was prescient? _____

8. Who received an accolade? _____

9. Who regarded someone as an anomaly? _____

10. Who fought bias? _____

 CONCISE WRITING: Make the following passages more concise, using no more than the number of words suggested.

---

1. That business in all probability would not have come to grief if the person who owned it had been more moderate in the consumption of alcohol.   (*Cut to about 15 words.*)

2. She can tell jokes that will have the place in an uproar without showing any emotional or personal involvement whatsoever. (*Cut to about 9 words.*)

_____

3. Those who are inclined to make the most favorable interpretation of events see the proposed granting of forgiveness for past offenses as a remedy that will cure all ills.   (*Cut to about 8 words.*)

_____

4. The people in the courtroom were overwhelmed with shock when the witness admitted that the evidence that he had given when he first took the witness stand had been made up for the purpose of deception.   (*Cut to about 15 words.*)

_____

5. In looking back over past events, we realize that the constitution of our club has on many an occasion been altered by modifications, additions, or deletions.   (*Cut to about 12 words.*)

_____

6. The proposal to finance trips to foreign countries for political appointees by dipping into funds that have been set aside for repairs is an example of a lack of foresight.   (*Cut to about 16 words.*)

_____

7. To tell the truth, I was disappointed that a speaker with so continuous and ready a flow of words as you have was almost unable to say a single word in support of the motion that I had made.   (*Cut to about 18 words.*)

_____

CLOSE READING: Read the following statements. Then answer questions 11–20.

STATEMENTS

In 1500, because of alleged misrule, Christopher Columbus, Governor of Hispaniola, was replaced by a new appointee and sent back to Spain in chains.

Cato the Elder, a Roman political leader, repeatedly declared that "Carthage must be destroyed" because he considered it the greatest threat to Rome.

In Shakespeare's *Richard III*, the monarch continues to fight on foot after his horse is killed, and cries, "A horse! a horse! my kingdom for a horse!"

Cesar Chavez improved the lives of migrant farm workers by organizing them and persuading the growers, who at first resisted, to sign contracts with them.

King Lear bequeathed his entire kingdom to his older daughters, Goneril and Regan, foolishly disinheriting Cordelia, the youngest, who truly loved him.

After fifteen months in a French prison, Charles Darnay was tried and found innocent, only to be rearrested a short time later.

In the novel *Roots*, Alex Haley traces his family's experiences back through many generations of American slavery to their remote ancestors in West Africa.

It never occurred to Amanda Wingfield that her daughter Laura was a truant from the private business school she was supposed to be attending.

When Mr. Lapham was unsure he could fill Mr. Hancock's order, Johnny Tremain, his young apprentice, settled matters by saying, "We can do it, Mr. Hancock."

One arduous task imposed on Hercules was to clean the Augean stables, which housed three thousand oxen and had been neglected for thirty years.

QUESTIONS

11. Who was viewed as an archenemy? _____

12. Who was superseded? _____

13. Who did not benefit from a parent's munificence? _____

14. Who had a noisome assignment? _____

15. Who reconstructed the lives of forebears? _____

16. Who offered an extraordinary incentive? _____

17. Who was not cognizant of a deception? _____

18. Who usurped someone else's prerogative? _____

19. Who enjoyed an ephemeral release from captivity? _____

20. Who initially did not capitulate? _____

 BRAINTEASERS: Fill in the missing letters, as in 1, below.

---

1. The United Nations took immediate steps to halt the carn **a g e** .

2. In our album, we keep the photos that we **c __ __ __ ish**.

3. Unbiased people show no __ __ __ __ **iality**.

4. Here is a cool drink to **assu _ _ _** your thirst.

5. **Inebri _ _ _ d** people may not be able to maintain their equilibrium.

6. The team that is trailing has an **un _ _ _ ny** ability to make a comeback.

7. Bitter words were spoken; the debate was **ac _ _ _ onious**.

8. Merchants reduced prices to **di _ _ _ _** themselves of excess inventory.

9. The **pur _ _ _ _ ed** gem has been recovered, but the thief remains at large.

10. Darkening clouds may **port _ _ _** the approach of a storm.

11. The play fascinated many but it did not **int _ _ _ ue** me.

12. I can't believe the excuse; it sounds so **_ _ _ lausible**.

13. Little of the beach is left; most of it has been **e _ _ _ _ d**.

14. Tourists climbed to the observation tower to **contemp _ _ _ _** the city's skyline.

15. **B _ _ _ _** yourselves; the news may shock some of you.

16. People with explosive tempers are quick to take **umb _ _ _ _**.

17. Some were **d _ _ _ _ ed**; others were not intimidated.

18. We like bright red tulips; others find them **os _ _ _ tatious**.

19. Current prices are **vola _ _ _ _ _**; nobody knows where they will go next.

20. We were **_ _ _ _ founded** by the recent surprising developments.

Vocabulary Index

bold type = lesson word; light type = synonym

Pronunciation Symbols

ə	banana, collide, abut
'ə, ˌə	humdrum, abut
ᵊ	immediately preceding \l\, \n\, \m\, \ŋ\, as in battle, mitten, eaten, and sometimes cap and bells \-ᵊm-\, lock and key \-ᵊŋ-\; immediately following \l\, \m\, \r\, as often in French table, prisme, titre
ər	operation, further, urger
'ər- 'ə-r	as in two different pronunciations of hurry \'hər-ē, 'hə-rē\
a	mat, map, mad, gag, snap, patch
ā	day, fade, date, aorta, drape, cape
ä	bother, cot, and, with most American speakers, father, cart
ȧ	father as pronounced by speakers who do not rhyme it with bother
au̇	now, loud, out
b	baby, rib
ch	chin, nature \'nā-chər\ (actually, this sound is \t\ + \sh\)
d	did, adder
e	bet, bed, peck
'ē, ˌē	beat, nosebleed, evenly, easy
ē	easy, mealy
f	fifty, cuff
g	go, big, gift
h	hat, ahead
hw	whale as pronounced by those who do not have the same pronunciation for both *whale* and *wail*
i	tip, banish, active
ī	site, side, buy, tripe (actually, this sound is \ä\ + \i\, or \ȧ\ + \i\)
j	job, gem, edge, join, judge (actually, this sound is \d\ + \zh\)
k	kin, cook, ache
k̲	German ich, Buch
l	lily, pool
m	murmur, dim, nymph
n	no, own
ⁿ	indicates that a preceding vowel or diphthong is pronounced with the nasal passages open, as in French *un bon vin blanc* \œⁿ-bōⁿ-vaⁿ-bläⁿ\

ŋ   si**ng** \\'siŋ\\, si**ng**er \\'siŋ-ər\\, fi**ng**er \\'fiŋ-gər\\, i**nk** \\'iŋk\\

ō   b**o**ne, kn**ow**, b**eau**

ȯ   s**aw**, **a**ll, gn**aw**

œ   French b**oeu**f, German H**ö**lle

œ̄   French f**eu**, German H**öh**le

ȯi   c**oi**n, destr**oy**, s**aw**ing

p   **p**e**pp**er, li**p**

r   **r**ed, ca**r**, **r**a**r**ity

s   **s**our**c**e, le**ss**

sh   with nothing between, as in **sh**y, mi**ss**ion, ma**ch**ine, spe**ci**al (actually, this is a single sound, not two); with a hyphen between, two sounds as in death**'s-h**ead \\'deths-ˌhed\\

t   **t**ie, a**tt**ack

th   with nothing between, as in **th**in, e**th**er (actually, this is a single sound, not two); with a hyphen between, two sounds as in knigh**th**ood \\'nīt-ˌhu̇d\\

<u>th</u>   **th**en, ei**th**er, **th**is (actually, this is a single sound, not two)

ü   r**u**le, y**ou**th, **u**nion \\'yün-yən\\, f**ew** \\'fyü\\

u̇   p**u**ll, w**oo**d, b**oo**k, c**u**rable \\'kyu̇r-ə-bəl\\

ue   German f**ü**llen, h**ü**bsch

ūe   French r**u**e, German f**üh**len

v   **v**i**v**id, gi**v**e

w   **w**e, a**w**ay; in some words having final \\(ˌ)ō\\ a variant \\ə-w\\ occurs before vowels, as in \\'fäl-ə-wiŋ\\, covered by the variant \\ə(-w)\\ at the entry word

y   **y**ard, **y**oung, cue \\'kyü\\, union \\'yün-yən\\

ʸ   indicates that during the articulation of the sound represented by the preceding character the front of the tongue has substantially the position it has for the articulation of the first sound of *yard*, as in French *digne* \\dēnʸ\\

yü   **you**th, **u**nion, **cue**, **few**, m**u**te

yu̇   c**u**rable, f**u**ry

z   **z**one, rai**s**e

zh   with nothing between, as in vi**si**on, a**z**ure \\'azh-ər\\ (actually, this is a single sound, not two); with a hyphen between, two sounds as in ga**zeh**ound \\'gāz-ˌhau̇nd\\

\\   slant line used in pairs to mark the beginning and end of a transcription: \\'pen\\

'   mark preceding a syllable with primary (strongest) stress: \\'pen-mən-ˌship\\

ˌ   mark preceding a syllable with secondary (next-strongest) stress: \\'pen-mən-ˌship\\

-    mark of syllable division

( )   indicate that what is symbolized between is present in some utterances but not in others: *factory* \\'fak-t(ə)rē\\